NAVIGATING
FINANCIAL
CHOICES

NAVIGATING
FINANCIAL CHOICES

A YOUNG ADULT

GUIDE TO EDUCATION,

WORK, AND MONEY

KAY L. O'DIAM

Gold Rim
PUBLISHING

Navigating Financial Choices: A Young Adult Guide to Education, Work, and Money
Copyright © 2025 by Kay O'Diam

All rights reserved. No portion of this book may be reproduced, stored in a retrieval system, or transmitted in any form or by any means—electronic, mechanical, photocopy, recording, scanning, or other—except for brief quotations in critical reviews or articles, without the prior written permission of the author.

NO AI TRAINING: Without in any way limiting the author's and publisher's exclusive rights under copyright, any use of this publication to "train" generative artificial intelligence (AI) technologies to generate text is expressly prohibited. The author reserves all rights to license uses of this work for generative AI training and development of machine learning language models.
No AI was used in the creation of this book or its cover.

Cover design by Miblart, Ukraine

Library of Congress Cataloging-in-Publication Data

O'Diam, Kay, 1957—, author.
Title: Navigating Financial Choices: A Young Adult Guide to Education, Work, and Money / Kay L. O'Diam.
Description: 240 pages—First Edition. | Dayton, Ohio: Gold Rim Publishing, 2025. Summary: A book to help young adults make informed decisions about their choices in education, work, and money, and understand how their thoughts impact their results.—Provided by publisher.
Identifiers: LCCN 2025918007 | ISBN: 979-8-9925371-0-9 (hardcover) | ISBN: 979-8-9925371-1-6 (e-book) |ISBN: 979-8-9925371-2-3 (paperback)
LC record available at https://lccn.loc.gov/2025918007

Printed in the United States of America

Disclaimer

Kay L. O'Diam is not a licensed financial planner or attorney. The information contained in this book is for informational purposes only and is not a substitute for professional accounting, tax, or legal advice. Under no circumstances will any blame or legal responsibility be held against the author or publisher for any damages, reparation, or monetary loss due to the information in this book either directly or indirectly. Readers are responsible for their own choices and results.

Dedication

I dedicate this book to the young people who were not taught how to make good financial decisions. This dedication is especially for the youth in the foster system, specifically those who were not given an opportunity to learn about financial topics before aging out and being forced to live independently. The Adoption and Foster Care Analysis and Reporting System (AFCARS) estimates that in 2021, 391,000 children were in foster care in the United States. During that same year, approximately 19,130 youth aged out of the system and were on their own.

Contents

Introduction 1

THOUGHTS

1. What's Thinking Got To Do With It? 7
2. Is My Programming Faulty? 9
3. Do I Really Need an Attitude Adjustment? 11
4. Gotta Have It 18
5. What's Coffee Got To Do With It? 22

EDUCATION

6. What Makes Me Special? 31
7. How Do I Get Educated? 36
8. The College Conundrum 43

WORK

9. How Do I Get a Job? 55
10. How Do I Keep the Job and Advance My Career? 63

MONEY

11. I Work Hard for the Money 75
12. Benefits 78
13. Taxes on Earned Income 88

14. Money That Works Hard for Me 101
15. Where to Grow Money 104
16. Formula to Make Money Grow 109
17. What is Debt? 121
18. How Do Loans Work? 124
19. Credit Scores 132
20. Big Ticket Items: Buying and Leasing 138
21. The GPS of Finances 148
22. You Snooze, You Lose! 156
23. Net Worth: What's the Big Deal? 173
24. Protecting What You Have 181

MAKE IT HAPPEN

25. Roadmap to Success 197
26. You've Got This! 205

NOTES 210
ACKNOWLEDGEMENTS 211
PUZZLE ANSWERS 212
GLOSSARY 218
RECOMMENDED RESOURCES 230

Introduction

It's time to start living the life you've imagined.

—HENRY JAMES, American Author

My primary reason for writing this book is to share information about money with teens and young adults, although others who have not been taught much about money may also benefit from the content. I was inspired to write this book after my daughter had shared a financial booklet I wrote for one of my workshops with a foster teen. The young woman was excited to learn about money. She shared it with her caseworker, who contacted my daughter to see if it was published so they could get copies to use with other teens in the foster care system.

Money can be a tough subject for people of all ages. In addition to trying to understand the financial terms and calculations, finance can be an emotional topic many people don't want to discuss. Society often uses money to judge a person's worth, which can create a lot of anxiety. Our financial status determines where we live, what we wear, and even what we eat. Don't feel bad if you don't really understand how money works. No one is born knowing. For most of us, we only learn what our parents or caretakers teach us. We can all agree that everyone needs money, so like it or not, it's part of everyday life. Unfortunately, most schools don't teach us about financial subjects.

I have a degree in accounting and have worked in accounting and finance for over forty years with various companies such as a bank, a certified public accounting firm, a law firm, a veterinary practice, an oil and gas company, and various Department of Defense contractors. I have also worked in human resources for over twenty-five years. Before semi-retiring, I was the vice president of finance and business administration for an aerospace manufacturing company. I am currently working part-time as a financial consultant for a software company. I have always enjoyed teaching and motivating people and eventually became a CTA certified life coach. I was a facilitator for DivorceCare, DivorceCare 4 Kids, and a motivational speaker and workshop presenter for Catholic Social Services, where I coached transformation and financial skills.

But I learned the most about personal finances when I was an unemployed, single parent struggling to support myself and three children. It is extremely scary to have no job and worry about whether you can feed your family and keep a roof over their heads. In this book, I will share the methods I used to gain control of my own finances and teach my children and many others through coaching and workshops. While I think it's important to understand financial terms and how our financial systems operate, I think the most important aspect of making wise decisions is understanding our own thinking. Therefore, I will be discussing how our thoughts affect our choices.

Throughout the book, you will find different boxes of content. The Sum It Up boxes will provide a quick recap of the material and the Brainstorm questions will be a guide to help you think about your own situation. The Did You Know boxes will present additional information relevant to the topic discussed and the Deeper Dive sections are for readers who want to deepen their understanding of the content. Each section will also have crossword puzzles for review. In addition, there will be a glossary at the end of the book for quick reference and a list of recommended resources to continue your learning.

We'll also take a closer look at some of the big money decisions you might face. *How do I get a job? What should I say to get hired by a potential employer? Do I need to go to college? How do I decide if I can afford something? How much should I save? Where should I put my money? What do all these financial terms mean? Why should I care about my credit score?*

This book is intended to be used as a reference for questions that come up in the future or for when you need some encouragement. You will not find any get-rich-quick schemes here. Regardless of how much or how little you knew before picking up this book, I hope you will take away new, helpful information. Understanding money shouldn't just be for people of privilege, it should be for everyone.

THOUGHTS

1

What's Thinking Got To Do With It?

*Confidence comes not from always being right,
but from not fearing to be wrong.*

—PETER T. MCINTYRE, painter and author from New Zealand

Most books and workshops about money talk about managing it. Money, in and of itself, is easy to control. Money doesn't have a mind of its own, and therefore, doesn't do anything until we make a choice. So, what we really need to talk about is how to manage our thoughts about money so we can make better financial decisions.

If we constantly make bad choices with our money, it won't matter how much we learn, we will still struggle. Our financial decisions are the result of what we have read, experienced, and learned. We rely on this programming to help us. It's similar to a computer. If there is an error in the software, we won't get the results we expect. No amount of positive thinking, understanding terminology, or following instructions will give us the correct answer. It's the same with us. If we have faulty programming from everything we've learned over the years, merely talking about financial terms and budgets isn't going to be helpful. So we'll start by examining how we think.

Whether we like it or not, we are all products of our environment. Things we see and hear as children help shape us into the adults we become. This early programming formed our paradigms, or belief systems, about everything from people, education, music, and food preferences to politics, religion, social programs, and the environment. It also formed our ideas about money. These influences often operate in the background, in our subconscious mind, without our awareness of how they affect our thoughts and ultimately, our decisions.

Most of us are familiar with phrases such as, "Money doesn't grow on trees," or "Money is the root of all evil." My mother was raised by her grandmother, who raised five children during the Great Depression of the 1930s. One phrase I heard often from my mother (and I'm sure she heard from her grandmother) while growing up was "We can't afford it."

We pass down phrases about money from one generation to the next, as well as generalizations about groups of people. And unfortunately, we often define ourselves based on generalizations held by society. For example, you might think that you will always be poor because you are a single parent, lack a college education, or live in a certain neighborhood. These untrue, self-limiting thoughts should be avoided; they will hold you back from reaching your full potential. Never let others define you. No matter what your background or current financial status, you can improve your situation! It might not be easy to make changes, but if you are willing to work for a better life, you can have one.

2

Is My Programming Faulty?

Progress is impossible without change, and those who cannot change their minds cannot change anything.

—GEORGE BERNARD SHAW, Irish playwright, critic, and political activist

One reason it can be difficult to change the way we make decisions about money is because programming exists in our subconscious mind. The activity in the subconscious mind goes on without our awareness—such as breathing, blinking, and swallowing. We often arrive at destinations without consciously thinking about the different steps we took to get there. Sometimes we don't remember the journey because our mind was basically on autopilot. To change our behavior with money, we need to reprogram the subconscious mind, which doesn't use logic like the conscious mind does. It does not analyze whether something is right or wrong, it simply accepts whatever you say. If you keep saying you have money problems or that you've always struggled with money, the subconscious mind will accept this and make decisions to support your belief.

The subconscious mind also filters what gets through to the conscious mind. For example, if I believe, based on things I have heard, that Taylor Swift is sweet and kind, whenever I see her, I will subconsciously look for sweet and kind behavior to support my belief. A person who believes Taylor Swift is arrogant and rude will subconsciously look for arrogant and rude behavior to support his or her belief. That is why two people can meet the same person and come away with two completely different opinions about what kind of person they met. By nature, we do not like to be wrong. When we cannot find support for a long-held belief, we feel uncomfortable; the evidence is not consistent with what we believe to be true. Because we need our beliefs to be in line with factual proof, our subconscious will filter out things that do not support them and this happens without us being aware of what the subconscious mind is doing.

The state of your life is nothing more than a reflection of the state of your mind.
—DR. WAYNE DYER, American self-help author and motivational speaker

If we know that the choices we make about money are rooted in our subconscious mind, how do we go about making changes? Awareness is the first step. We need to pay attention to our thoughts and question them. Ask yourself what you've heard, read, or experienced that contributed to that belief. When we discover a belief that may be responsible for some of our poor choices, we need to make a conscious effort to have new thoughts that align with our goals and make the necessary choices to achieve them. When we change the way we consciously think, our subconscious mind will accept this new thinking as our truth. This applies not only to money but to everything in life. When we live life with an open mind and question our beliefs, we will find that our subconscious mind will help us make better choices.

A mind is like a parachute. It doesn't work if it is not open.
—FRANK ZAPPA, American musician, composer, and bandleader

3

Do I Really Need an Attitude Adjustment?

Insanity is doing the same thing over and over again and expecting different results.

—ALBERT EINSTEIN, theoretical physicist, Nobel Prize winner

Because our subconscious mind is programmed by what we see, hear, read, and experience, we may have developed some unhelpful thoughts and attitudes. If we want different results, we need to be open to new ways of thinking that will lead to better choices.

Self-Sabotaging Behavior

If we lack confidence in our abilities or feel we don't deserve to succeed, we may subconsciously sabotage ourselves. We might experience this when we get a promotion at work and don't feel we have the qualifications to do the job. At times, this occurs when we achieve success and don't think we are worthy. Another way we can hurt ourselves is when we buy things to soothe anxiety. Maybe we are frustrated because we don't have enough money to buy a house. Instead of saving money for a downpayment, we buy things we don't need. Rather than recognizing that our failures are due to our own programming, we may launch into *victim thinking*. Whenever we start to have thoughts that undermine our goals for our future, we need to challenge these beliefs and make a conscious effort to change our thinking.

Victim Thinking: Giving Away Our Power

Forces beyond your control can take away everything you possess except one thing, your freedom to choose how you will respond to the situation.
—VIKTOR E. FRANKL, Austrian Holocaust survivor, psychiatrist, philosopher, and author

When we think we have no control over what happens to us, we might blame a certain person or circumstance. This is victim thinking. When we feel that someone or something else is responsible for our situation, we give away our power to whomever or whatever we blame. It's easier to claim we are a casualty because we can attribute our mistakes and failures to others. Unfortunately, this kind of thinking holds us back. If we go through life with a victim mindset, we lack the courage to work for what we really want in life. Would we rather be miserable—never getting what we want—or take responsibility for creating the life we would like to have? If we have a victim mentality, we have an *external locus of control,* which means we feel helpless because we think everything that happens to us is due to something outside of us. Psychologist Julian Rotter developed the concept of "locus of control," which refers to the degree to which individuals believe they can control events in their lives.

We are all more motivated and happier when we have an *internal locus of control.* With an internal locus of control, we keep the power to affect our outcomes and create a better life. Once we understand we always have a choice in how to respond to our circumstances, we take back our power. Our decisions always determine our results.

Challenges

The difference between a successful person and others is not a lack of strength, not a lack of knowledge, but rather a lack in will.

—VINCE LOMBARDI, NFL football coach

This brings us to another thought that can hold us back. If we view challenges as obstacles, we can feel defeated. Maybe we don't want to put in the work or are afraid of failing. We may want to give up when we face difficulties. For this reason, we sometimes resort to victim thinking instead of facing hurdles head on.

If we want to succeed in our efforts to improve, we need to view obstacles as opportunities. When we push through, we find that even if we fail, we learn. The challenges often make us stronger and provide insights. Hard things are necessary for us to grow and become better. Think of how a butterfly works tirelessly to emerge from a cocoon; the struggle is critical to strengthen its wings to fly. Successful people aren't born that way. We may think it is simple for them because we did not see the persistent efforts they made to accomplish their goals. Remember, in life the test comes first, then the lesson. If you are not facing challenges, you are not learning and growing! Embrace opportunities; they are the steppingstones to your achievements!

BRAINSTORM:

What thoughts are holding me back?

....

....

....

Now that we have examined some of the types of thinking that can interfere with our success, let's discuss thoughts that can cause worry or frustration. When we have worrisome thoughts, we should question them. Are they facts or only thoughts? My friend's sister had to have a biopsy to determine if her tumor was malignant (cancerous) or benign (non-cancerous). My friend was in a complete state of panic, dwelling on what she would do without her sister. While I understand this situation can be very upsetting, her thoughts about her sister's diagnosis were still only thoughts because she didn't have the facts yet. It was also possible her sister's tumor could be benign. Since she didn't know which thought was accurate, I suggested she *choose* to focus on the good outcome. She decided to think about a positive outcome, which helped her relax while she waited for the results. It turned out her sister's tumor was benign and posed no health risk.

I've had a lot of worries in my life, most of which never happened.
— MARK TWAIN, American author and humorist

Negative thinking can cause us to feel frustrated and sometimes, even angry. One of the most powerful ways to handle negative thinking is to reframe your thoughts and focus on what you are thankful for. For example, last summer I went down into my basement to check on my laundry and saw that my basement had flooded. My initial thoughts were *"This is awful! I don't have time to clean this up, and now I'll have to pay to have someone clear the drain."* Of course, these thoughts were negative and well, okay, I will admit, whiny. So how did I flip the script and think positively with gratitude? I told myself I have a sewer line that could clog because I have a home. I have laundry in my home because I have indoor plumbing. Indoor plumbing made me think about how thankful I am to have an indoor bathroom and that I don't have to use a smelly outhouse. I think you get my drift.

When I was a facilitator for DivorceCare, I was working with people who were devastated by their situations. We started each session by sharing something good that had happened to them during the week. Initially they struggled to think of anything, but eventually they started to share. At first everyone shared something bad, but put a positive spin on it. Soon they no longer dwelled on the bad things they experienced, but eagerly shared the good things that happened. Often we are so focused on what is negative, we overlook all of the positive things we have to be thankful for.

According to *Psychology Today*, "Gratitude is perhaps the most important key to finding success and happiness in the modern day." If you do an internet search, you will find numerous studies about how gratitude improves mental health, acts as a natural anti-depressant, enhances physical health, improves sleep, boosts self-esteem, and even changes your brain to give you a permanent grateful and positive nature.

BRAINSTORM:

What are some worrisome thoughts I have? Are they facts, or just thoughts?

....

....

....

What are some ways I can reframe my thoughts so I don't get so frustrated or angry when my circumstances are disappointing?

....

....

....

What am I thankful for?

....

....

....

*Everything negative—pressure, challenges—is all
an opportunity for me to rise.*

—KOBE BRYANT, Former American professional basketball player

Developgoodhabits.com cites a number of examples of people who faced big challenges but achieved success because they didn't give up.

- **Michael Jordan**, one of the greatest basketball players of all time, was cut from his high school team.
- **Jerry Seinfeld** froze during his first comedy act and was booed off the stage within three minutes.
- **Stephen Spielberg**, director of *Indiana Jones*, *Jurassic Park*, *ET*, and many other award-winning films, was rejected from film school three times.
- **Elvis Presley** was fired after his first performance. His manager said, "You ain't goin' nowhere, son. You ought to go back to drivin' a truck."
- **Stephen King**, bestselling author, was rejected thirty times before his first book, *Carrie*, was published.
- **Albert Einstein** had speech difficulties and was thought to be mentally handicapped as a child.
- **George Lucas** was rejected by three studios before *Star Wars* was finally made.
- **Walt Disney** was fired from his job because he "lacked creativity."

- **Oprah Winfrey** was publicly fired from her first job as a TV news anchor.

I have missed more than 9,000 shots in my career. I have lost almost 300 games. On 26 occasions I have been entrusted to take the game-winning shot, and I have missed. I have failed over and over again in my life. And that is why I succeed.
—MICHAEL JORDAN, American businessman and former professional basketball player

4

Gotta Have It

He who buys what he does not need, steals from himself.

—SWEDISH PROVERB

Sometimes we make poor spending choices because we don't distinguish between needs and wants. A need is something necessary to survive, like water, food, clothing, and shelter. When you live at home, your parents probably pay for most of your needs. However, when you live independently, your needs will be your responsibility.

Start by identifying which items fit into the need category and estimate what each of these items costs. Keep in mind that different areas of the country have a different cost of living, which means the cost for the same item can be quite different depending on where you live. It's a good idea to create a spending plan or a budget to make sure you have enough money each month to cover your needs. See the chapter *The GPS of Finances* for more details.

When you own or rent a home, you also need utilities, which are services such as electric, gas, oil, water, sewer, phone, internet, and trash. I include phone and internet as needs even though they are not necessary for survival. In modern life, internet and phone access is becoming a necessity for daily activities. This can include needing the internet for schoolwork or a phone for an emergency situation.

If you rent, some utilities may be included in your monthly rent payment, but usually, you are required to pay at least some. The cost of these services may vary based on the amount you use. For example, during certain seasons, you may use more electricity due to heating and cooling. Many utility companies are willing to do a level billing. This means they will estimate the cost for the entire year and divide it into twelve months, and you pay the same amount every month. At the end of the year, they will adjust your bill up or down to correct the estimate to the actual cost. Paying the same amount can be helpful when creating a budget to know exactly what to expect each month. If you've never had an account with the utility company before, you may be required to pay a deposit to open one. The deposit will be returned to you later if you pay your bills on time.

Other needs to be considered for your household are consumer staples (essential products) and insurance. Consumer staples are items such as food, beverages, clothing, toiletries, laundry detergent, dish soap, and cleaning products. These items are needed on a regular basis.

Another cost to consider is insurance. Insurance will protect you from losses due to fire, theft or other events. Renter's insurance will cover your belongings when you rent, and homeowner's insurance will cover your belongings and your dwelling if you own your home. Refer to chapter on *Protecting What You Have* for more information on insurance.

Unless you are in a situation where you can walk everywhere you need to go, you will need to factor in an amount for transportation. If you have a car, you should estimate how much you will need for parking, gas, and auto expenses such as oil changes, auto maintenance, auto insurance, driver's license, registration fees, and a payment if you have a car loan or lease. If you don't have a car, estimate what you will need to spend on other transportation, such as a train or bus pass. For more information on leasing or buying a car, refer to the section on *Big Ticket Items: Buying and Leasing.*

You may also have additional needs, such as tuition and books for school or uniforms for work. If you are moving out on your own for the first time, you may also need to plan for furnishings and household goods such as bed sheets, blankets, towels, dishes, and silverware.

Whenever you spend money on needs, ask yourself what the outcome will be if you do not pay for the particular need. For example, let's say you really want to go to a concert (want), so you skip your rent payment (need) and use the money for concert tickets. What might be the consequence of that choice? You will probably have to pay a late fee, or if the choice is repeated, you could be evicted from your home.

DID YOU KNOW?

Inflation is a general rise in prices for goods and services. This can happen when the cost of producing goods and services (wages, materials, and shipping), rises and/or there is a rise in demand–more buyers want goods and services–usually because taxes and interest rates are lower so they have more money to spend.

Deflation is a general decrease in the prices of goods and services. This can happen when demand drops (fewer buyers want goods and services–usually because taxes, interest rates, and unemployment are high–so they have less money to spend. Companies often lay off employees because sales of their products or services are down and they have less money to run their business.

Stagflation is when inflation is high, economic growth is low, and unemployment is high.

Supply and Demand is how the supply of goods and services compares to the demand for goods and services. When supply is high and demand is low, prices go down. When demand is high and supply is low, prices rise.

Recession is a period of economic decline which can cause demand to decrease, unemployment to rise, and businesses to lose profits.

Depression is like a recession but much longer (usually many years) and much more severe. Depressions can be caused by a stock market crash, bank closures, natural disasters, and changes in politics or society.

Federal Reserve is the central bank of the United States. It acts to stabilize our economy. In an effort to reduce inflation, they will tighten monetary policy by raising interest rates (called a rate hike) to make it harder to buy goods and services, which helps reduce demand. If the economy is shrinking, they will usually reduce interest rates, making money more available, which usually has the effect of increasing demand. Simply put, they try to maintain economic growth while keeping prices stable and unemployment low.

5

What's Coffee Got To Do With It?

We talked about needs, now let's talk about wants. A want is something that is not required to sustain life. Wants are not harmful unless we spend so much on them that we don't have enough money for our needs or for emergencies that might arise

A want could be something like going out to eat when you already have food at home. Many of my workshop participants listed cable television as a need, but it is a want. We do not need cable or even regular television service to survive.

A want can also be something added to a need. For example, my son needed a new pair of tennis shoes, which at the time cost about $35, but he wanted a more popular brand that cost $65. I told him I would pay for the need ($35), but he could get the $65 shoes if he paid for the want ($30). He decided he would use $30 of his own money and buy the more expensive shoes.

Spending a few dollars here and there doesn't seem like a big deal, but little purchases can add up quickly. Impulse buys are especially hard to resist—that's why stores put small items at the checkout and display items throughout the store. Maybe when you're out shopping, you see a pair of boots you like. You didn't have boots on your list, but you are tempted to buy them. Patience is required for success. Think about waiting to see if you still want them next week. Consider saving money and purchasing them after you have saved enough. Stores often have clearance sales at the end of a season to prepare for next season's merchandise. If you wait until the end of the season, you can often purchase items at discounted prices. For example, I needed a warm winter coat and saw one at the store for $200. It was a well-made coat, but more than I wanted to spend. I saved my money, and when I checked back at the end of the winter season, it was on sale for $80. I still use it today, twenty-four years later.

Quality is also something you should consider before making a purchase. If you buy something of inferior quality because it costs less but wears out quickly, you end up spending more. It is better to save for what you want and only buy good quality.

Over the years I have accumulated a lot of stuff. I don't want to be featured on the show *Hoarders*, so I have a rule. If I buy something new, I must donate or sell something I already own. If I were considering a new pair of boots, I would ask myself which pair of shoes can go in order to get the boots. When I think of it that way, I often end up deciding against the purchase.

Lastly, ask yourself how many hours you would need to work to get this want. Let's use our example of boots. If you earn $20 per hour and the boots cost $100, that means you would have to work five hours to have enough money to buy those boots. Would you be happy if your employer gave you those boots instead of money for five hours of work?

Earlier we discussed how society can influence our buying decisions. When we allow others to define us, we can get derailed trying to live up to their standards or prove them wrong. Isn't this the real reason we try to "Keep up with the Kardashians" and buy houses, cars, or clothes we can't afford? We want to be *perceived* as someone society views with higher regard. Instead of comparing ourselves to others, it is more productive to focus on our own situation and how much better we are today than we were yesterday.

*If we aren't careful, our children will come down with 'affluenza,'
a disease that causes them to confuse wants and needs.
We need to teach our children what my grandmother taught me:
Think twice about spending money you don't have on things
you don't need to impress people you don't like anyway.*
—MICHELLE SINGLETARY, author and personal
finance columnist for *The Washington Post*

Although it is fine to purchase wants within reason, we must be careful that our wants do not derail our financial plan. Before purchasing a want, make sure you have enough to cover your needs and some funds set aside in case of an emergency. If you have savings goals, make sure you have those covered too before buying a want.

What is Your Latte Factor®?

I have often heard in workshops that participants think getting ahead financially is hopeless. Then we talk about the *latte factor®*. David Bach, author of *The Latte Factor*, coined the phrase. Basically, it refers to giving up a frequent, small purchase (a want) and putting that money toward savings instead. Maybe you don't buy coffee or lattes, but there is probably some small purchase you make each week that you could give up. All the participants in my workshops were able to think of something that they could easily give up or buy less frequently so they could start saving. One woman said her family could do pizza night every other weekend instead of every weekend and that would save about $50 per month. The group was excited to learn this concept because it was a small sacrifice that could pave the way for them to start saving and improve their financial situation. So, I ask you, what is your *latte factor®*?

SUM IT UP

Before You Buy

Is this a want or a need? (Do you need it to survive?)

Needs

- Can I afford not to pay for this need?
- What will be the outcome if I don't?

Wants

- Do I currently have enough money for my needs and a potential emergency?
- If I buy this, will I still be able to meet my financial goals?
- Can I save for this and buy it later?
- Am I able to wait and buy this at the end of the season when it may be on sale?
- Is this good quality?
- Do I already have enough of this item? What item would I be willing to part with to get this item?
- How many hours would I have to work to get this item? Would I be happy to work that many hours for this item instead of money?
- Do I want to buy this just to impress others?

BRAINSTORM:

MY NEEDS	
Description	Est. Cost

MY WANTS		
Description	Est. Cost	Is this a Latte Factor®?

#1 THOUGHTS

ACROSS:

1. We feel empowered if we have this locus of control
5. When negative thoughts interfere with our success or peace of mind we can choose to do this
7. What does *Psychology Today* say is perhaps the most important key to finding success and happiness?
9. Where our programming exists (2 words)
13. A small purchase you can give up to save money (2 words) Hint: coined by David Bach
14. With this type of thinking we give away our power and blame someone or something for our failures
15. Cable TV is this
16. If we wait and buy at the end of this we often save money
17. Some people buy things they don't need just to _____ others

DOWN:

2. We feel helpless if we have this locus of control
3. We should always have money set aside for this
4. To be successful we need to think of obstacles or challenges as _____
6. Buying this may cost more up front but saves money in the long run
8. When deciding whether to spend money for this, always ask yourself what the outcome will be if you don't
10. Sometimes we subconsciously hinder our own success
11. Required for success
12. Never allow this to judge you

EDUCATION

6

What Makes Me Special?

*Decide upon your major definite purpose in life
and then organize all of your activities around it.*

—BRIAN TRACY,
Canadian-American motivational speaker and author

Unless you have inherited money, you will most likely need to work. Before you search for a job, decide on a career path, or determine whether you need to go to college, let's think about the kind of employment suited for you. When you choose a career in line with your natural inclinations, your job will be more gratifying. You may have heard someone talk about being *in a flow state* when they are working. Flow happens when you are passionate about what you are doing. It feels effortless, you are fully engaged, and time flies. Wouldn't you like to have work you find enjoyable, in part, perhaps because it suits you well? Maybe you can think of competencies you possess, such as musical or athletic skills. Or you might struggle to recognize what your talents are. Let's look at some ways to identify your gifts.

First, think about what you enjoyed doing as a child. A child's play is like practice for adulthood. Maybe you loved being physically active or enjoyed art, music, writing, or building things. Or perhaps you pretended you were a teacher, a nurse, a parent, or a business owner. These things don't always foretell what you will do for a career, but they can tell a lot about what you enjoy. My oldest son loved to play computer games and works as a senior software engineer. My daughter was an avid reader; she now teaches Latin and is a freelance book editor. Childhood activities do not always dictate your career path, but they can give you some insights into what types of jobs may be a good fit.

Next, think about what your passion is. If money were no object, what would you like to do even if you didn't get paid? What types of things inspire you? Which activities do you lose track of time while doing? What actions taken by others do you find motivating? Ask people who know you well what they think you gravitate toward. What are you naturally good at? Perhaps you are a talented athlete, musician, or artist. Or you might naturally be good at organizing things or people, listening to others, being persuasive, or cooking. Are you talented with hairstyles or fashion? Do math, science, or language come easily to you? Maybe you are not exceptional at something yet, but you have a strong interest and learn skills quickly in certain subjects.

After you decide what your gifts are, think about careers that utilize these skills. Do you think you could make money doing this? Would this field inspire you every day? Is there someone you know who does this job? If so, ask to meet with them to talk about their work or maybe visit them on the job. Perhaps you could volunteer for an organization that does what you would like to do.

There are a number of personality assessments to help suggest which jobs would be a good fit for you. Myers & Briggs is one of the most common. I took the Myers & Briggs assessment and found it to be quite accurate for me. Career Explorer by Sokanu is a free online assessment that is quite good, too. There are also other assessments online. Some are free, some charge a fee, and some require a subscription. Be sure you know how much it will cost and read all the policies and privacy notices before signing up for anything.

The internet also has videos of "A Day in the Life" of different careers. I would recommend that you focus on the ones created by Indeed, as they are much more professional and, in my opinion, a more accurate representation of what it is like to work in that career. They also show the skills needed to succeed, how to begin, and the pros and cons of the job.

Remember that each one of you is unique. Think about it—no one on the planet, now or in years past, has had the exact same experiences combined with the exact same talents you possess. That makes each individual person special. When you use your natural abilities, you are positively contributing to the greater good.

Imagine your favorite song. Each song is made up of different notes. If one note—the D, for example, was left out, the song wouldn't be the same. Without it, you might not even recognize the song. Every note matters.

If you think you are too small to make a difference,
try sleeping with a mosquito in the room.
—AFRICAN PROVERB

Just as each note in the song is needed, each person's contribution to their community is important. Whether you are a doctor, server, lawyer, sanitation worker, or teacher, everyone's role matters. Imagine what your neighborhood would be like if no one was willing to collect garbage. We all contribute to the well-being of the whole community. Therefore, everyone's contribution counts.

The eye can never say to the hand,
'I don't need you.' The head can't say to the feet,
'I don't need you.' In fact, some parts of the body that seem weakest
and least important are actually the most necessary.
—BIBLE (NIV), 1 Corinthians 12:21-22

BRAINSTORM:

What did I enjoy as a child?

....

....

What do I enjoy now?

....

....

....

Who do I admire and why?

....

....

....

What are my skills or talents?

....

....

....

What are my passions?

....

....

....

WHAT MAKES ME SPECIAL?

What would I enjoy doing even if I didn't get paid?

....

....

....

What careers seem like a good fit for me?

....

....

....

Do I know anyone who works in this field?

....

....

....

What type of education do these careers require?

....

....

....

7

How Do I Get Educated?

If you are not willing to learn, no one can help you.
If you are determined to learn, no one can stop you.

—ZIG ZIGLER, Author and motivational speaker.

Now that we have talked about ways to choose a suitable vocation, let's discuss how to obtain the skills necessary to succeed in that career. There are basically two main ways to learn: a formal education, and an informal education. Let's explore the differences.

Formal Education

One way to acquire knowledge is through a formal education. Some of the common degrees you can get from a college or university are a vocational degree or certificate, associate's degree, bachelor's degree, master's degree, and doctoral degree. Master's degrees and doctoral degrees are obtained through higher levels of instruction; we will focus on programs that typically take four years or less. If you don't have the money or time in your schedule to attend school full time, you can attend part time. This will take longer but may be more achievable for some. Also, many colleges and universities offer options to attend in person or online.

The following descriptions offer some general information as well as an estimate of how much time it takes to complete certain educational programs. Prices will vary by state and school—public state school versus private institution. A public state school is normally less expensive than a private school.

Vocational Certificate

Investopedia describes a vocational degree as "an academic certificate awarded to students who have completed the degree requirements for a specific trade or career." This type of education can take from two months to two years on average and upon completion, you are ready to work in that field. Some jobs that you can get with a vocational certificate are practical nurse, massage therapist, dental assistant, paramedic, and plumber.

Associate's Degree

There are two types of associate's degrees. One is known for being a university parallel. If you plan to get a bachelor's degree (four-year program) and want to save money, you might consider taking the first two years at a community college. You may choose a major, but it is not required. These degrees typically take 40-60 credit hours—a credit hour is the number of hours of class time required per week. For example, if you sign up for an English class that is three credit hours, you should expect to spend three hours per week in class. You should also expect to spend two to three hours of study outside of class for each credit hour. Most colleges and universities consider you a full-time student if you are taking twelve hours or more per semester. Upon completion, you will earn an associate's degree of arts (AA) or associate's degree of science (AS). Then you may transfer the credits you earned to the school where you plan to finish the other two years. Usually only the classes offered at the freshman and sophomore levels in the four-year program will transfer.

The other type of associate's degree, called the associate's degree in applied science (AAS), is referred to as the career path. If your goal is to get as much training as possible so you can start your career, this may be the preferred option for you. This type of degree does require a major. Your curriculum includes the advanced classes you would take at a four-year college as a junior or senior. Often when you compare the career-related classes offered in the associate's degree program, they are the same as the classes offered in a four-year degree. The AAS degree does not require as many general education credits and can be completed more quickly. The primary focus is on the classes that relate to your career. These degrees require 60-100 credit hours. Some examples of AAS fields include accounting, information technology, graphic design, dental hygiene, criminal justice, and automotive technology.

Bachelor's Degree

Bachelor's degrees are either bachelor's degree of arts (BA) or bachelor's degree of science (BS). They will include completion of classes in your major as well as a number of required general education credits, which are classes that do not directly relate to your major. A bachelor's degree is normally around 120 credit hours.

> *Formal education will make you a living; self-education will make you a fortune.*
> —JIM ROHN, American motivational speaker and entrepreneur

Informal Education

An informal education is a great way to learn and improve skills. For this type of learning, you select what you want to study and guide your own learning process. The internet and the public library are excellent resources. At the library, you have access to a vast array of books on a wide variety of subjects. In addition, the internet has numerous websites and videos on a variety of topics. Following creators of YouTube videos, bloggers, or subscribing to newsletters published by organizations or schools is a good way to find out about seminars and pick up additional information. If you don't have internet at home, you can access the internet at your local library at no charge.

If you want to learn something and provide a service to others, the internet has videos that are five minutes long and some that are hours long. For example, if you want to do bookkeeping for clients, you can learn about QuickBooks online. You can even take an online course and get certified in QuickBooks. There are a number of websites that will connect freelancers (people working on their own) with people who need the services they provide. Some examples are Fiverr, Toptal, Jooble, Freelancer, and Upwork.

Friends are also a valuable resource. If you have friends who know a skill you want to learn, ask them to teach you. It is also helpful to build your own library of books you can refer to for valuable information. Much of what I have learned is from my own personal library of experts, such as Steven Covey, Jim Rohn, Jack Canfield, Brian Tracy, Dr. Wayne Dyer, Robert Kiyosaki, Angela Duckworth, and Brené Brown, along with books on topics like Microsoft Excel.

DID YOU KNOW?

Many massive open online course (MOOC) providers let you audit college courses for free. Two examples are edX and Coursera. You can access the classes and most course materials at no cost, or you can sign up to get a certificate of completion for a fee. I used Coursera to take a class at Yale and get a certificate for a cost of $50. When you want to obtain high quality knowledge for free or get a certificate and do not need college credit, this is a great way to learn.

On-the-Job Training

On-the-job training (OJT) is one of the best ways to pick up new abilities. Some companies are known for their excellent training programs. Search the internet for companies known for their training programs and see if any interest you. When I finished school, I had one offer in accounting from a small company and another offer from General Motors' headquarters that paid about thirty percent more. I was tempted by the money, but my dad held a position with GM and was bored while he was there. Because it was such a large company, he did one small segment of cost accounting every day and found it to be monotonous. I wanted to be challenged and decided the smaller company would provide better opportunities. It turned out to be a good decision. I viewed the thirty percent difference in pay as the cost of furthering my education. I had an entry level job, and every day, I would complete my work as quickly as possible, then go around and ask others in the department if there was anything I could do to help. I acquired valuable experience. After three months, the person who prepared the financials for our Texas division had a baby and decided she would not return to work. Our boss promoted me to the position because I had been assisting her and knew what to do.

Another way to get on the job training is through an internship. An internship is a short-term position, usually entry-level, that is designed to help you gain skills and experience in a specific field. Some internships are paid, and some are unpaid. Internships allow a student to obtain work experience and training in a field. Some internships also offer college credit. Although most internships are for college graduates, adults can also do an internship. This may be something for an adult to consider if they become unemployed or want to switch careers. Employers will ask about gaps in work on your resume; an internship would be one way you could fill that gap. If interested in an internship and you are a college student, you can ask the career services at your school. Adults can ask people within their network, their alma mater (school where they graduated) or people they know through a professional association. Websites like LinkedIn, Glassdoor, Internships.com, and Internmatch.com are also useful resources for finding an internship.

When you change the way you look at things,
the things you look at change.
—DR. WAYNE DYER, American author and motivational speaker

Volunteering

I can't say enough about the benefits of volunteering. Serving others is the best way to boost your confidence and self-esteem. Volunteering can also expose you to many different types of work and provide opportunities to learn new skills. For example, when I volunteered to work for a charitable organization that repaired houses in Kentucky, I learned how to use power tools to build and make repairs.

I took management courses in college and attended numerous seminars over the course of my career, but the best management training I ever had was when I volunteered as an administrator for a youth program managing thirty volunteers. These volunteers worked with seventy kids ranging in age from preschool to high school. Some volunteers and members of the church wanted to end the program because of the kids' bad behavior. When you manage volunteers, you must develop the leadership skills to inspire them to follow you and believe in the vision that you are trying to accomplish. Unlike in the workplace, volunteers do not care about your title. You can call yourself whatever you want, and it makes no difference to them. They do not care if you threaten to give them a write-up, a suspension, or a termination. They are not employees, and they are not getting paid, so if they don't like the way things are going, they leave and don't come back. Anyone who's worked in a volunteer organization knows that having volunteers leave can be devastating to the program. And all these considerations also applied to the kids. They don't care about titles and knew they couldn't be kicked out, per the organization's rules.

As a result, one challenge was trying to find ways to encourage good behavior from the kids and have them show respect to the adult volunteers. On the other hand, I needed to find ways to inspire patience and understanding in the adult volunteers working with the kids. I learned that the most important thing a leader can do is listen to understand. Listening promotes effective communication among the adults and kids, which supports the mission of the program.

My advice to all new managers is to treat the people who report to you like they are volunteers and use inspiration to lead. People are a company's best assets. You don't want your company's best assets to leave the building and never return. It is the role of the manager to provide the necessary resources, support, and guidance to help them be the best they can be. This is the education I acquired through my volunteer experience. My college classes and management seminars never taught this.

8

The College Conundrum

I will study and get ready and someday my chance will come.

—ABRAHAM LINCOLN, 16th U.S. president

Now that we have discussed various ways to get educated, let's look at things to consider when deciding whether to attend college. College is a big commitment of both time and money, so this is a decision that requires careful thought.

First, make sure you are ready to go to college. By that I mean, not everyone is ready to jump into college right out of high school. I have seen too many young people attend college right away (usually because they think it's expected) and waste a lot of time and money because they weren't ready yet. College is a lot of hard work. If you aren't ready to commit to making the effort, you might consider taking a gap year to think about what you want your future to look like. My oldest son was adamant that he was never going to attend college. After high school, he found a full-time job and was content with working. Years later, while serving in the National Guard, he decided on a career that required a college degree. He worked part time, attended college full time, and was able to use the GI Bill (benefits created to assist American military veterans) to help with his expenses. He completed his bachelor's degree and went on to obtain a master's degree. Don't feel you have to go to college right after high school. Every person's path is different, and you should do what is right for you.

Next, consider what level of education is needed for the vocation you have chosen. Research different schools that offer what you need and compare costs. If you need a four-year degree, can you complete the first two years at a community college and save money? Will you need to pay extra for your living expenses? If you need to borrow money for your education, consider what kind of pay you could expect in this field and how much the student loan payments would be. Some careers require a college degree, but the pay is very low, which makes it difficult to pay for college debt. Most people who are making payments on a student loan will tell you it feels like a huge burden for many years. Don't let the cost of student loans discourage you from pursuing the career of your dreams, but make sure you understand the financial commitment you're making.

Some people work while they go to college and pay for their tuition as they go. Others may use their savings, such as money in a 529 plan. A 529 plan is a tax-advantaged account designed to be used for educational expenses. As long as the money is used for educational expenses, there is no income tax when you make withdrawals. Money saved in a 529 plan that is not used for education can now be converted to a Roth retirement account. There are certain limitations, so check the IRS rules.

DID YOU KNOW?

If you don't have the money but decide you want a formal education, financial assistance is available. Scholarships are usually based on merit instead of need, and grants are usually based on need rather than merit. Scholarships and grants do not normally need to be repaid. You can apply for financial aid, such as a grant, *work study funds,* or a loan through *FAFSA*. Depending on your situation, you may be eligible for *subsidized federal loans* (loans that do not charge interest until six months after graduation) or *unsubsidized federal loans* (loans that begin charging interest as soon as you borrow). Check with your school's financial aid office, your school's website, or get more information at https://www.usa.gov. Some states offer *Post Secondary Enrollment Options* (PSEO), programs that pay the college tuition for students to attend college while still in high school and earn credits for both (must meet requirements for eligibility). Starting in the fall of 2025, some colleges are going to offer free tuition to qualifield students. Search "colleges offering free tuition" for more information.

You may also be eligible for opportunities such as the GI Bill, which offers help with college expenses to soldiers and veterans as a benefit of their service. Some states also have programs to assist veterans. In addition, many employers offer educational assistance to their employees. For example, McDonald's offers educational assistance to employees who have completed ninety days of service and work at least fifteen hours per week. McDonald's recently opened this assistance to the family members of employees as well. Amazon also pays for employees' tuition through their Career Choice program. IBM established a program in 2011 called P-Tech, a public education model that provides high school students from underserved backgrounds with the academic, technical, and professional skills and credentials they need for competitive STEM jobs. This is available in twenty-eight countries.

During one of my workshops, a recent college graduate broke down crying because she had graduated from a state college with a four-year degree, could not find a position in her field of study (because she lacked experience), and had $40,000 in student loan debt. Sometimes, the economy makes it difficult to find a job in the career you chose even when you have a degree. Remember, the job market is always changing. If this happens to you, consider working in a different field until a job in your field becomes available. You can learn and develop skills in any occupation. Don't stop learning and don't give up!

Before you look for a job or decide to pursue a formal education beyond high school, you should know about a current trend known as degree inflation. In 2017, Harvard Business school released a report, "Dismissed by Degrees—How Degree Inflation is Undermining U.S. Competitiveness and Hurting America's Middle Class." Burning Glass Technologies, a research partner on this study, analyzed twenty-six million job postings and found a discrepancy between the percentage of job postings requiring a bachelor's degree and the percentage of people currently in that position that hold a bachelor's degree. They call this discrepancy the degree gap.

The Harvard research showed consistent survey results across many industries and indicated that non-college graduates with experience do as well or nearly as well as college graduates. In addition, non-college graduates tend to stay with a company longer and show higher levels of engagement.

Degree inflation should inform rather than discourage you. Use this information to develop a strategy when seeking employment. If you do not have a degree and your potential employer requires one, you may want to see if someone in your network can get you an interview even though you don't have a bachelor's degree. Often a hiring manager (the boss for the open job) will tell human resources what he or she needs. If human resources was told the candidate needs a bachelor's degree then they will not consider anyone without the degree. However, if you can find a way to speak directly with the hiring manager and demonstrate how much you know, the manager may decide you are qualified even without the degree. Refer to *How Do I Get a Job?* for more information.

> *Obstacles don't have to stop you. If you run into a wall,*
> *don't turn around and give up. Figure out how to climb it,*
> *go through it, or work around it.*

—MICHAEL JORDAN, American businessman and former NBA player

If you are someone who doesn't have the opportunity to earn a bachelor's degree, do not be discouraged. You are not alone. According to the U.S. Census Bureau (as of 2021) 37.9% of adults in this country have a bachelor's degree or higher. The following people didn't attain a college degree and they didn't let it stop them from achieving their dreams. These people prove that a college degree is not the only way to obtain knowledge and achieve your goals. A degree doesn't define how smart you are or what you can contribute to society.

Ted Turner—Founder of CNN, **Bill Gates**—Co-founder of Microsoft, **Mark Zuckerberg**—Founder of Facebook, **Wright Brothers**—Inventors of the airplane, **Thomas Edison**—*Inventor* of the light bulb, **Steve Jobs**—Co-Founder of Apple, **Oprah Winfrey**—Media Mogul, **Walt Disney**—Founder of Walt Disney Co., **Stephen Spielberg**—Movie Director (*ET, Raiders of the Lost Ark*, and *Jurassic Park*), **Frank Lloyd Wright**—Iconic architect, **Jack Dorsey**—Twitter, **Travis Kalanick**—Uber, **Milton Hershey**—Founder of Hershey Chocolate, **Ralph Lauren**—Fashion Designer, and **Tyler Perry**—Movie Producer

You can find more at www.smartandrelentless.com.

BRAINSTORM:

What type of education will I need?

....
....
....

How do I plan to get this education?

....
....
....

Do I need to go to college? If so, am I ready yet?

....
....
....

Am I able to get assistance through scholarships, grants, work study, employee education assistance, or loans?

....
....
....
....
....

If so, what type(s) and how do I apply?

....
....
....
....

These are the places of education I have researched:

....
....
....
....

What expenses would I need to cover (such as books, housing, and tuition)?

....
....
....
....

How much do I estimate these costs to be?

....
....
....
....

How do I plan to pay for the education I need?

How long do I expect this to take?

How do I plan to get experience in this field?

#2 EDUCATION

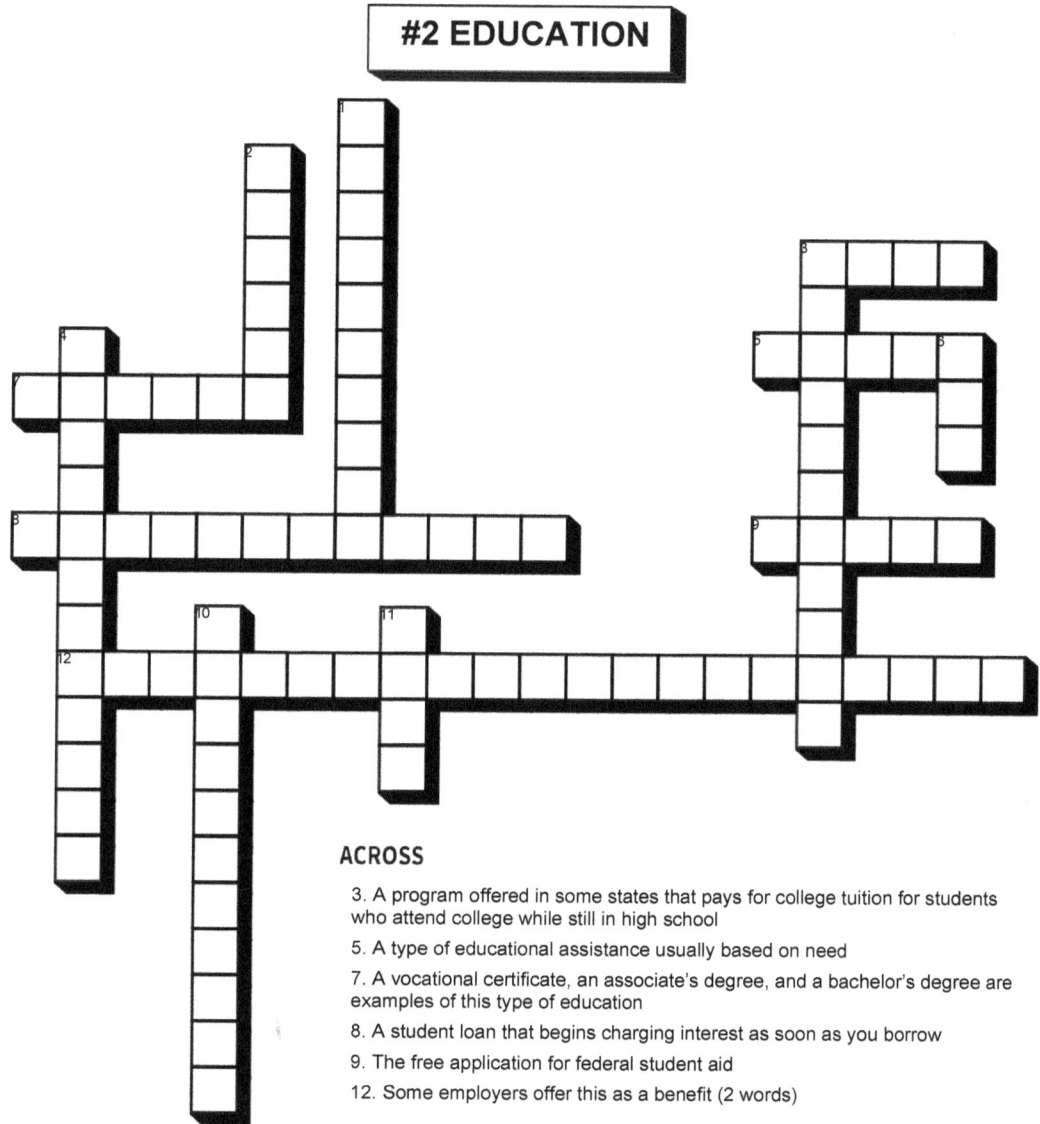

ACROSS

3. A program offered in some states that pays for college tuition for students who attend college while still in high school
5. A type of educational assistance usually based on need
7. A vocational certificate, an associate's degree, and a bachelor's degree are examples of this type of education
8. A student loan that begins charging interest as soon as you borrow
9. The free application for federal student aid
12. Some employers offer this as a benefit (2 words)

DOWN

1. A student loan that does not charge interest until six months after graduation
2. Assistance for soldiers and veterans (2 words)
3. Something of yours you should consider when deciding what job is a good fit for you
4. A type of informal education
6. A 529 Plan is what type of advantaged plan to help save for educational expenses?
10. A type of educational assistance usually based on merit
11. EdX and Coursera are examples of free or low cost online courses also know as

WORK

9

How Do I Get a Job?

You must take personal responsibility. You cannot change the circumstances, the seasons, or the wind, but you can change yourself.

—JIM ROHN, American motivational speaker, and entrepreneur

We examined how to decide what career is a good fit for you and we reviewed various ways to obtain an education. Now it's time to talk about how to get a job. When preparing to accomplish anything in life, you need a strategy. Before mapping out a plan, do your homework. Knowing what human resources and hiring managers are looking for is a good place to start when looking for a job.

Employers strive to find candidates by identifying the skills required for a position. Human resources, a hiring manager, or a recruiter will then advertise the opening, often by posting a job description, along with the skills the applicant should possess, on sites like Indeed, Glassdoor, and LinkedIn. Part of your homework is to read a lot of these listings to see what employers want. Pay close attention to the job duties (the employer's needs) and the minimum and preferred requirements (what the applicant needs to know so they can meet the employer's needs). You can also call on a local employer to see if they are hiring. The types of positions you typically find this way are entry level positions. This is more common in the hospitality industry (hotels, restaurants) and retail stores.

Make a list of what skills listing employers are looking for, such as "proficient in Microsoft Excel." These are the skills you need to incorporate into your study plan if you want to get hired for this type of position. Next, focus on the job duties or a list of the employers' expectations. For example, the employer may list a necessary skill as proficient in Excel, but in reading the job description, you see they want data sorted and analyzed to help them make decisions in their business. It is critical that you understand the employer's needs and how you can meet them before you draft a resume, cover letter or go to an interview (there are many books and websites that deal with how to construct cover letters and resumes, so we will not cover that in this book).

To better understand the potential employer, learn about their business by reading their website and news articles about them. I worked in HR for over twenty-five years, and one question I always asked was "What do you know about our company, and why do you want to work here?" You would be surprised how many candidates did not have an answer to that question. One of my biggest pet peeves was resumes (or candidates during an interview) that stated the reason for applying was "to gain experience, further my career, or make more money." Those may be *your* objectives, but that doesn't address how you will meet the needs of the employer. Imagine going into a car dealership and saying you are looking for a used car that costs around $20,000 and the salesperson shows you a Ferrari SF90 Spider Convertible with a price tag of $583,950. "This car is perfect for you," he says, "because I will get a huge commission!" The salesperson isn't focusing on what you need and can afford; he is only concerned about what he will get out of the deal. You need the salesperson to show you a car that fits your specific needs and budget. It is the same with employers. They are looking for someone who can solve their problems and be an asset to their company.

People you know may also be able to help you find employers who are hiring. Networking is a terrific way to gain access to a position you are interested in. Finding a job is sometimes as much about who you know as what you know. Don't be afraid to ask people you know for assistance. They may have contacts in your field of interest or know someone who may be able to help you score an interview. Sometimes if you can speak directly with the hiring manager and show you have the necessary skills, you can get around the degree requirements listed in the job posting. To network, get to know a wide circle of people. Friends, neighbors, and acquaintances are all important in building a network. Treat everyone with respect and before you know it, you will have a network. You never know who may be able to help you find and obtain a position.

Speaking of networks, make sure you never post inappropriate things on your social media. Employers often look at your profiles to decide if you are someone they want to bring onboard.

BRAINSTORM:

What skills do I need to get a job in the field I am interested in?

....

....

....

How do I plan to obtain those skills?

....

....

....

Who do I know that could be in my network and help me in my career?

....

....

....

What companies have I applied to? What do I know about them, and why do I want to work there?

....

....

....

DID YOU KNOW?

A ghost job is a job posting for a position that doesn't exist or has already been filled. Here are some things to look for to see if the job posting is real:

- ➢ Does the job description detail all the responsibilities of the position? If not, it is probably a ghost job.
- ➢ Was the job also posted on the company website? Most of the time, only real job openings are posted on their own website or social media page.
- ➢ Is there any indication of how long this job has been open or how many applicants have applied? If it was posted over a month ago or has lots of applicants already, it is probably a ghost job.

Interviewing

Once you are invited to an interview, then what? First, dress for the occasion. You do not need to dress formally, but at least wear business casual—a button-down shirt, sweater or blouse, nice slacks (no holes, sweatpants, or pajama pants), a knee-length dress or skirt, sport coat, cardigan or blazer (optional), closed toed shoes, and simple accessories. Try to dress appropriately; this is not a date or social outing. What you wear should show you are taking the interview seriously. If you do not have appropriate clothes and cannot afford to buy them, shop at a thrift store. People often donate business attire.

Arrive at the interview at least ten minutes early. Often, employers will ask you to complete an application. Take a copy of your resume and references so you have the information to complete any form. You should be ready to begin the interview at the scheduled time. Punctuality will impress the interviewer and shows that you will be an employee who comes to work on time.

Being prepared is also knowing why you want to work there and how you can address the company's needs. They may ask questions about the type of work environment you prefer, how you handle stress, and what you like to do in your free time—search Google and You Tube to get an idea of sample interview questions. If you have a gap in employment on your resume, be sure you can explain why—maybe it was due to unemployment, going back to school, health, or family issues. Be sure to make eye contact when you speak. Often an interviewer will ask if you are applying for other jobs and what pay range you're looking for. I recommend you say you are considering other opportunities, and that pay is negotiable. Companies rarely decide what to pay based on what a potential candidate says they want. They already have a budget in mind for the position. If you say a salary higher than their budget, you may take yourself out of the running. If you go lower or at the low end of their budget, they may offer less pay. I suggest only discussing pay *after* they make a job offer to you.

At the end of the interview, always give a firm handshake, look the interviewer in the eye, and thank them for their time. Afterward, always send a thank-you note or email. This is not only a way to thank them, but also reminds them why you are interested and how you can help meet their needs. Hardly anyone takes the time to follow up with a thank you anymore. Whenever I had two equally qualified candidates, the one who made the effort to send a thank you would get the job offer. It shows an employer that you don't merely do the minimum required but go the extra mile.

BRAINSTORM:

Do I have a resume and references?

....

....

....

For each job I applied to, how can I meet the company's needs?

....

....

....

What is appropriate attire for an interview?

....

....

....

If you get a job offer, you want to know about everything included, also known as the total compensation package. This includes pay and benefits like insurance, paid vacation, a retirement plan, etc. Refer to *Benefits* for more information. The benefits a company offers you have value and should be considered when deciding about compensation. For example, let's say Company A offers you $25 an hour, but the only benefit they offer is one week of paid time off. Company B offers you $23 an hour but they also offer health insurance (company pays 80% of the cost of your health insurance), a 401k plan with a 4% match—a match of 4% means the company will contribute what you contributed up to 4% of your gross income, and two weeks of paid time off. Now look at the offers side by side in the table below. Which is the better offer?

Pay and Benefits	Company A		Company B	
Regular Pay (40 Hour work week)	(51 * 40) *25	51,000	(50 * 40) * 23	46,000
Paid Time Off	(1 * 40) * 25	1,000	(2 * 40) *23	1,840
Health Insurance		0	(1,000 * 12) *.80	9,600
401k match up to 4%		0	(46,000+1,840) * .04	1,914
Total Compensation		52,000		59,354

Figure 9.1 Comparison of Total Compensation

As you can see in Figure 9.1 Comparison of Total Compensation, the value or total compensation package offered by Company B is $7,353.60 more than the total compensation package offered by Company A, and you only have to work fifty weeks for Company B because they give you two weeks of paid time off. With Company A you would have to work fifty-one weeks because they only give you one week of paid time off. Benefits make a big difference, and companies offering them usually take better care of their employees. You should also consider taxes. In the section on *Benefits*, we'll discuss how different benefits are taxed differently, which can affect how much pay you take home. Keep in mind that getting a pay increase or working more than one job can change your tax bracket. Search federal tax brackets at https://www.irs.gov. You add the gross pay you get from a raise or from multiple jobs, and get a total from all jobs. Then look at the tax brackets for the current year to estimate your taxes. For an example and more information, refer to the section on *Payroll Taxes*.

In *How to Get Educated?—On the Job Training*, I encourage you to consider any learning opportunities you may receive from a company when deciding whether to accept an offer. Although you do not want to present this reason during the interview (make the interview all about the employer), on-the-job training and educational assistance are benefits you don't want to overlook.

BRAINSTORM:

List each company that has made you an offer, then fill out the information for each to compare the total compensation packages. Be sure to include any training that the company will provide either through on the job training or educational assistance. Reference the Comparison of Total Compensation Package earlier in this chapter for an example.

PAY AND BENEFITS	COMPANY:		COMPANY:	
Regular Pay				
Paid Time Off				
Health Insurance				
Retirement Match %				
Other				
Other				
Other				
Total Compensation				

10

How Do I Keep the Job and Advance My Career?

I know of no more encouraging fact than the unquestionable ability of man to elevate his life by conscious endeavor.

—HENRY DAVID THOREAU, American naturalist, essayist, poet, and philosopher

So far, we have talked about how to learn skills and find a job. Now we will focus on what you can do to stand out, get noticed, and advance in your career. Remember, your learning shouldn't stop after you land the job. Advancing your skills is critical to advancing your career. In addition to learning, many behaviors will serve you well in being regarded as an invaluable employee. Some employees want to do the bare minimum to keep earning their paycheck. If you want to advance your career, you must demonstrate you are someone who goes above and beyond expectations. Again, think of how your skills match what your employer needs.

Opportunity is missed by most people because it is dressed in overalls and looks like work.
—THOMAS EDISON, American inventor and businessman

Show Up

It may seem strange that I list "show up" as something to do after you get the job. I graduated high school with a guy who was recognized for having perfect attendance throughout all twelve years of school. Some people didn't think he should get an award for just showing up. My father was an elementary school principal, and he thought it was one of the most important accomplishments to recognize. After all, no one ever achieves anything if they don't show up. You may not be the smartest or have the most important job, but when you consistently show up, people know they can rely on you.

Be Willing to Step Up

Be willing to help others or fill in where there is a need. Cross training (learning other job duties) is especially important to a company. If someone is out sick or leaves the company, they need someone who can fill in. If you remember, in *Informal—On the Job Training*, I suggested you treat each position as a way to increase your education. I shared how I turned down an offer for a higher paying position for more on-the-job training with my current employer. Make it your goal to add skills not in your job description and be the person your employer can count on when they need someone to help in another area.

Be Proactive

My parents didn't give us chore lists when I was growing up. We were expected to "see" what needed to be done. One evening, my dad asked why I had not washed the dishes, and I replied that no one told me to. "No one should have to tell you," he said. "You walked by a sink full of dirty dishes and could see they needed to be washed." As a child, I hated that practice, but when I entered the workforce, I continued this routine out of habit. At my first job, many workpapers for an upcoming audit needed to be prepared. After I finished my work (and anything else I could help with), I pulled out last year's workpapers as a sample and began preparing the workpapers for the current year's audit. My boss praised me and said the other people in the department had been there for years and never did anything before the last minute. She was surprised because I had only been there for a couple of months and she hadn't asked me to do it. I made a note to myself that being proactive is something that not only impresses parents, but also bosses.

People who are proactive anticipate a potential situation and take steps in advance to avert trouble, rather than responding to a problem after it has occurred. In other words, someone who is proactive is taking action to prevent fires while someone who is reactive is responding to fires already burning. To use your time wisely, you need to have a proactive mindset, which means anticipating things before they happen. Otherwise, you will waste a lot of time fixing things that shouldn't have happened in the first place. Someone who thinks proactively also anticipates management's questions before they ask, which helps management stay on top of issues.

Be Prepared

"Do your homework" means be prepared. Take time to understand the issue and do your research. If you have a meeting scheduled, prepare in advance. Anticipate the questions and have informed responses. Learn how to feel confident and comfortable speaking in front of a group. Be able to clearly state facts, as well as your opinions. If the company has a decision to make and you disagree with the other points of view, listen carefully. To effectively convey your point of view, you need to understand the opposition. You'll know that you understand when you can argue for their points as well as they can. If they do not feel that you grasp what they are saying, you will never be able to convince them you have a valid point to be considered. Once, someone told me they had complained to their boss because they never won an argument with a certain co-worker (we will call her Olivia). They meant it as a derogatory comment. However, his boss responded, "In all the years I have worked with Olivia, she has always done her homework. If you can't convince her to see your point of view, then you obviously didn't do yours." Occasionally, someone may present a compelling argument, and you must be willing to pivot to help your team implement the best solution. Be someone who prioritizes finding and implementing solutions over always having to be right.

DID YOU KNOW?

Toastmaster International is a nonprofit educational organization that builds confidence and teaches public speaking skills through a worldwide network of clubs that meet online and in person. In a supportive community or corporate environment, members prepare and deliver speeches, respond to impromptu questions, and give and receive constructive feedback. It is through this regular practice that members are empowered to meet personal and professional communication goals. You can find more information at the website, https://www.toastmasters.org.

Be Professional

A professional is respectful even when others are not. I have witnessed adults in the workplace behaving like toddlers. They badmouth others, give coworkers the silent treatment, call names, gossip, swear, and whine. This type of behavior is very immature and should always be avoided at work.

People who resort to these tactics rarely advance in their career. Typically, they will blame others for why they never get promoted. Someone who accepts responsibility for mistakes and uses constructive criticism to learn and improve is going to earn respect and get noticed.

Be Honest

Be honest with everyone. For people to respect, listen, and follow your lead, they must trust you. Make truthfulness a habit. Don't participate in gossip. People who gossip to you will gossip about you and it erodes trust in the workplace. Have the courage to speak up when something is wrong and help make it better.

Be Willing to Dress for Success

Dressing for success doesn't mean you must wear expensive clothing. It means dressing for your role or the role you wish to have. If you are a mechanic, dress like a mechanic. If you have a position in an office, dress like the leaders in the office.

For example, I was considering someone on my accounting team for a promotion, but the CEO didn't think he was the right person for the job. I found this frustrating because he wasn't familiar with the employee's work. Then I observed the CEO talking to him like he was a young teenager, even though he was forty years old. The person I wanted to promote wore an untucked T-shirt and jeans to work. In addition, he wore a knit hat during the day and had an unkempt beard. I told my team member what I had observed and said if he was serious about the promotion, he should consider dressing for the position and tidying his appearance so he looked more like a professional accountant. Because we were a manufacturing company, our dress code permitted jeans and a T-shirt, so he wasn't breaking any rules. However, he was being considered for a role in management and would be representing the company in meetings with other business leaders. Therefore, upper management expected him to look like a professional. My team member began wearing button down shirts tucked into his jeans, and stopped wearing knit hats during the day. He also trimmed his hair and his beard. Shortly after that his promotion was approved. You don't have to wear expensive clothing to look well-groomed, but if you want to be considered a good fit for the job, your appearance plays a part.

Be Responsible

Be someone who takes responsibility for their mistakes. If you make a mistake and do not own up to it, people will lose respect for you. I have worked with people who always blame others. No one is perfect, and if you pretend to be, people will not believe you. When you do make a mistake, be willing to find a solution and fix it. Don't be someone who causes issues for other people to fix. That will not endear you to your colleagues.

Being responsible also includes having self-control at company functions or events. If alcohol is served (and you are of legal drinking age), limit yourself to one or two drinks and never get drunk. Companies can also be held legally and financially responsible for bad things that happen when someone drinks too much at a company-sponsored event. If you are someone who drinks, save it for time spent outside of company gatherings.

Be a Leader

Many people aspire to become "the boss." If you do become someone with a team reporting to you, remember that having the title doesn't mean people will follow you. Your role is not to be bossy. People will listen to those they trust and respect, whether they have a title or not. A leader is someone who instills trust, inspires others, and knows how to bring out the best in people. The person in charge needs to make sure the people reporting to him or her have the resources and support they need to succeed.

Asking others for input is also important. When people feel they are heard and their opinions are valued, they become more engaged and committed to their work. Performance also improves. Because not all people are the same, you can't necessarily treat everyone the same. For that reason, it is helpful to get to know each person that reports to you. Different people are motivated in different ways and respond to situations differently. You may need to treat each individually, but you must treat all fairly. And, if things go wrong, be prepared to take the heat; the leader is ultimately responsible.

If you have an employee who is a poor performer or does not follow the rules set for the team, it is critical that you address it immediately and document everything. Stop bad behavior in its tracks before your good employees become resentful and their performance begins to suffer. Allowing bad behavior may be interpreted as consent, which can make it more difficult to address later. If you have a team member who refuses to improve after you have addressed the issues, you need to terminate their employment. A bad actor on your team is like a disease that will spread and infect the whole team. Note that even an "at-will" employer (an employer that can end employment at any time for any reason) can still be sued for wrongful termination. To protect your company from a lawsuit and to avoid having to pay unemployment to someone terminated for cause (meaning they deserved to be fired due to their behavior) you must carefully document all unacceptable behaviors and the actions taken to address it.

For such leadership roles, how do you acquire the skills required? As I mentioned in *How Do I Get Educated?*, volunteer work is one of the best ways to learn. Developing the attributes of a good leader—regardless of whether that is your role—is a wonderful way to excel in the workplace. There are many good books on how to develop leadership skills. A few of my favorites are *Principle-Centered Leadership,* by Stephen R. Covey, *The 21 Irrefutable Laws of Leadership,* by John C. Maxwell, and *Leading at a Higher Level,* by Ken Blanchard.

Even if you don't aspire to have a leadership role, everyone should learn how to lead. Learn to become someone who is able to take charge when necessary. If there was an emergency, would you want everyone in the group to be a follower? Someone needs to be able to stand up and direct people to avoid a disaster. Learn how to think on your feet—think quickly under pressure—and be a problem solver.

SUM IT UP

How to Succeed on the Job
- Show Up
- Be Willing to Step Up
- Be Proactive
- Be Prepared
- Be Professional
- Be Honest
- Be Willing to Dress for Success
- Be Responsible
- Be a Leader

ACROSS:

3. A way to meet people who may be able to help you get an interview
6. A meeting between an employer and a potential hire
8. A non-profit organization that teaches public speaking
11. The pay and benefit package offered to a potential hire (2 words)
14. Always do this before an interview to find out about the company and know why you want to work there
15. These should always be considered along with pay before accepting a job offer
16. A job posting that isn't real
17. Always take this along with your references to an interview

DOWN:

1. After an interview always make _____ contact, give a firm handshake, and follow up with a thank-you email
2. Recommend you say this if asked during an interview what pay range you are asking for
4. Always act this way when on the job or at a company function
5. Usually listed in the job ad—what is needed to do the job
7. A good way to get experience
9. A person who plans ahead to avoid problems
10. Whose needs should you focus on during an interview?
12. Always consider these opportunities when considering a job
13. Always do this before a meeting

MONEY

11

I Work Hard for the Money

Things may come to those who wait,
but only the things left by those who hustle.

—ABRAHAM LINCOLN, 16th U.S. president

We have discussed how to get a job and advance in your career. Now let's look at the different types of income. *The Oxford Dictionary* defines income as money received, especially on a regular basis, through work or investments. The two main types of income are earned income and passive income.

Earned Income

Earned income is the money you get paid for working. If you don't work, you don't *earn* money. This type of income can be in the form of an hourly wage (including tips and bonuses), salary (including commissions and bonuses), or contract pay. Let's begin our discussion with pay for employees: hourly wages and salaries.

Hourly Wage

An hourly wage means you get paid a certain dollar amount for every hour you work. For example, if your hourly wage is $20 per hour and you work 2 hours, you get paid $40. If your hours vary each week, your income will also change. In the U.S., if an hourly employee works more than 40 hours in a week, the employer is required to pay extra for the hours over 40. If you make $20 per hour and work 41 hours, the extra hour will be at time and a half, also referred to as overtime—regular rate ($20) + half of the regular rate ($10) = $30). Your pay would be $830—$800 (40 hours x $20) weekly pay + $30 overtime pay (1 hour x $30). Many employers will require overtime hours to be approved beforehand.

Salary

Another type of pay is salary. Salaried employees normally get paid the same amount each week regardless of the hours they work. An exception to this rule is an employee who is considered non-exempt, which means if they work over 40 hours per week, they are entitled to be paid overtime for the extra hours worked.

Most salaried employees are considered exempt, which means they do not get paid overtime when they work more than forty hours per week. A salary for exempt employees is based on completion of the work assigned—or outlined in the job description. If an exempt salaried employee does not complete the work during the 40 hours, they can be expected to work extra hours with no additional pay. For more information on labor laws governing labor classifications—hourly, exempt salaried and non-exempt salaried,—overtime pay, etc. go to https://www.dol.gov.

Contract Labor

Another type of earned income is contract labor. Contract labor is when you do work for a person or a company, but you are not their employee.

It is still earned income because you are doing work to earn it. It is called contract labor because you have a contract, or an agreement with the person or business for whom you are doing work. Under this type of agreement, you are either paid an hourly amount for time worked or a set dollar amount for the completion of the job. The contract should also outline the scope of work to be performed, when payment is due, and how the contract may be terminated.

DID YOU KNOW?

The Department of Labor has rules about whether someone should be classified as hourly, non-exempt salary, or exempt salary. The classification determines whether an employee should be paid overtime. There is also a rule that an employer may not classify someone as a contractor if they treat them like an employee. Employers sometimes do this to avoid paying social security taxes, medicare taxes, and benefits. Human resources departments need to follow these rules. If they do not, the Department of Labor can investigate and assess fines for any wrongdoing.

12

Benefits

Now that we have discussed different types of earned income, we need to talk about the difference between gross income and net income. *Gross income* is your hourly wage or your salary. *Net income* is the amount of pay you take home. Some employers may offer benefits and withhold (take out) the cost or a portion of the cost from your pay. There may also be taxes withheld from your pay depending on how much you earn, where you work, and where you live. Because a contract laborer is not an employee, there are no benefits or taxes withheld from contract pay, although contractors are still expected to pay taxes which, we will discuss in *Payroll Taxes*.

The paystub shows the details of your gross pay, minus your share of any benefit costs and the taxes withheld to equal your net income. The net income, also called take home pay, is what will be paid to you, usually in the form of a check or by direct deposit into your bank account. See Figure 12.1 Paystub and Paycheck.

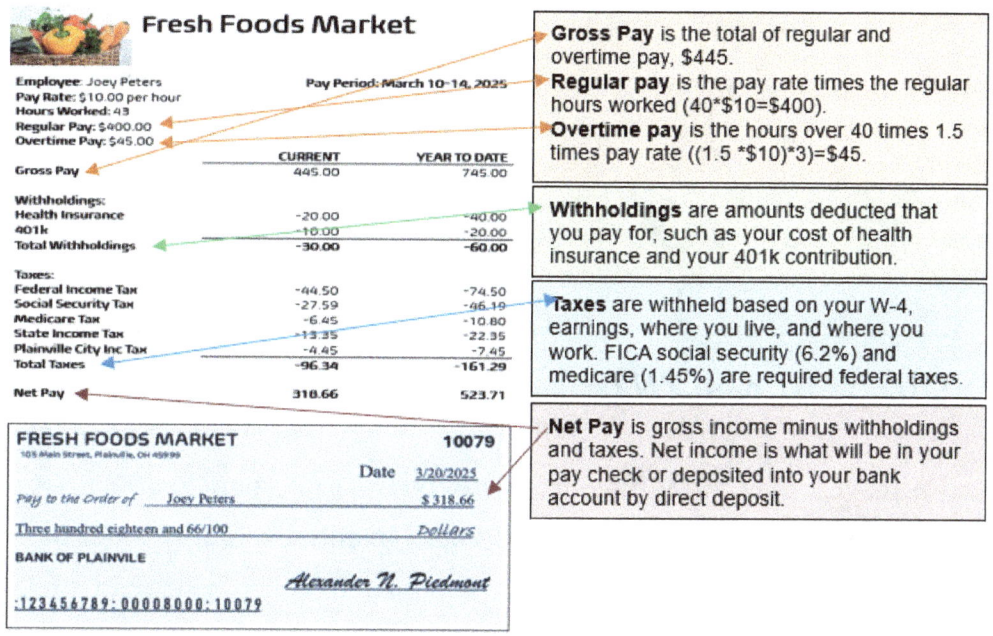

FIGURE 12.1 PAYSTUB AND PAYCHECK

To see if the federal rules about benefits and taxes have changed, go to https://www.irs.gov and search for the topic. To find updated state or local tax information, visit the website of your state or city. During the open enrollment period, your company's HR department should tell you of any changes being made to the benefits your company offers. Benefits can be taxed differently. For additional information, refer to the sections on pretax and post-tax benefits in *Types of Benefits* and *Payroll Taxes*.

Types of Benefits

Many employers choose to offer benefits to their employees as an incentive for the prospective hire to work for them instead of another employer. After you are hired, normally you will be given paperwork about your benefits and taxes on the first day of work or before. Many of the benefits offered to you are optional, and you can decide if you want to sign up for them. Some benefits will come at a cost to you, while the employer may partially or entirely pay for others. Still others may have an employer match, meaning the employer will contribute money for you to whatever benefit they are matching.

DID YOU KNOW?

Employers may be required by law to offer certain benefits, such as workers' compensation, unemployment insurance, family medical leave, and health insurance. These required benefits depend on the size of the company and federal and local state laws governing the company.

Workers' Compensation is to protect workers in case they get injured on the job. This is a tax paid by the employer.

Unemployment Insurance is another tax paid by the employer. This protects workers who have been laid off or terminated (due to no fault of their own), so they can collect unemployment while they look for a new job.

Family Medical Leave Act (FMLA) requires an employer to hold the job open for an employee that has a legitimate, family-related reason for taking time off work. There are rules about what qualifies, and not all companies are required to offer this.

The Consolidated Omnibus Budget Reconciliation Act (COBRA) is another benefit some companies are required to offer. This allows an employee who is no longer employed to be able to stay on their company's insurance plan for a period of time. The employee does *not* qualify if they were terminated for cause. The former employee pays 100% of the cost plus an administration fee. This is a limited time offer. For most people, coverage lasts 18 months, but there are some other qualifying events that may lengthen this coverage up to 36 months or 29 months, depending on the event.

Most benefits, like health insurance, have a benefit period of twelve months. This may be the same as the calendar year or it may be a different twelve-month period. Each year, benefits are reviewed and can change. Employees are asked to review the changes and make elections (choices) during the open enrollment period, which lasts for thirty days. This is the only time you can change certain benefits like health insurance, unless you have a qualifying event, such as divorce, death, marriage, loss of coverage, a new child, or change of address—speak to human resources at your work if you need to make a change. There are many different types of benefits, such as health insurance, college tuition reimbursement, retirement plan, bonuses, and paid time off.

Let's dive into a few of the more common ones. One benefit often offered by employers determines whether you get paid when you take time off for a personal reason or when you are sick. This benefit is called *paid time off* (PTO). PTO is the number of hours you can be absent for any reason (personal, vacation, or sick) and still get paid. Other companies may not call it PTO, but will designate a number of hours for vacation and a different amount of hours for illness. Regardless of whether they put the hours together and call it PTO or separate them by vacation and sick days, the basic calculation is the same. The benefit is for a set number of hours during the *benefit period* (a twelve month period of time). If your employer offers 40 hours of PTO, that means that you can take off up to

40 hours during that benefit period and still be paid. For example, if you were sick one day and missed 8 hours of work, you would get paid for the 8 hours missed and your remaining PTO hours would now be 32 (40-8). You should keep track of your PTO hours so you know how much you have remaining. Some employers will put it on your paystub, but if you have questions about your PTO hours, you should reach out to your human resources department.

The benefit period of your PTO depends on each employer. Some employers consider the benefit period for PTO the same as the calendar year while some have the year start with the anniversary of your hire date. Still others may have it correspond with the benefit period of your health insurance. After you use up your paid hours, you will no longer get paid for the time off. Employers that offer this benefit are also permitted to dock or withhold the pay of a salaried person if they exceed their PTO hours. For example, let's say a salaried person earns $1,500 each pay period, but takes off one day and has no PTO hours remaining. Their employer can deduct 8 hours of their pay for the time they were off. Employers can also require permission to take off for personal or vacation.

Unlike PTO, health insurance is a benefit that may come at a cost to you. Maybe the total cost of your monthly health insurance premium is $1000. The employer may pay 80% and require you to pay 20%, or $200 per month. The employer will pay the insurance company the full amount of the premium, and your share will be deducted from your paycheck. In this case, if you were paid twice per month, $100 would be withheld from each of your paychecks to cover your share of your health insurance benefit.

Because there are so many different types of health insurance policies offered by employers, this topic will not be covered in detail in this book. Speak with the human resources department at your company to get information about your specific plan.

> *There is a law that states health insurance must be affordable, and each year, the government puts a limit on what percentage of your gross pay is considered affordable for your share of the insurance premium.*

Some benefits are considered pre-tax, while others are post-tax. *Pre-tax* means the deductions for the benefits are deducted from your gross income before taxes are calculated (making your taxes lower). Benefits that are *post-tax* are deducted after the taxes are calculated (they do not reduce your taxes). Please note that tax laws and benefits can change. Ask your human resources or payroll department to learn which deductions are considered pre-tax and post-tax each year. Refer to the example in *Payroll Taxes*.

Pre-tax Benefits

Some examples of benefits that may be deducted from your paycheck before taxes (pre-tax) are your share of health insurance premiums, contributions you make to a health savings account, and contributions you make to a traditional 401k—retirement plan. The following list does not include all pre-tax benefits, but rather, some of the more common ones.

➢ **Section 125**(IRS tax code) such as a *cafeteria health insurance plan* which is a type of health plan that allows employees to choose which benefits they want to enroll in such as dental and vision and complies with Section 125 of the tax code. The portion of the premium withheld from your paycheck is considered pre-tax. *Not all health insurance plans qualify.* Ask the human resources department where you work. There is a law that states health insurance must be affordable, and each year, the government puts a limit on what percentage of your gross pay is considered affordable for your share of the insurance premium. For more information go to https://www.irs.gov/affordable-care-act/individuals-and-families/questions-and-answers-on-the-premium-tax-credit#affordability.

➢ *Health savings account (HSA)* is an account you are eligible to open if you are enrolled in a high deductible health plan (HDHP). With a high deductible health plan, you will pay more out of your pocket before insurance pays for any claims. For this reason, the IRS allows you to save money toward your medical expenses. Some employers give their employees an opportunity to open a health savings account where employees can contribute—EE-employee portion—to the account from their pay. These contributions are pre-tax. As long as you do not exceed the maximum contribution permitted by law, others can also contribute to your HSA account. Some employers will contribute to their employees' HSAs. Employer contributions—ER-employer portion—do not come out of your pay and are not taxable to you. If your employer does not offer to open an account for you, you can still open one on your own, and the contributions will still be tax-deductible. All of the earnings from the money you save in a health savings account are non-taxable too. However, the money may only be used for qualified medical, prescription drugs, dental, and vision expenses. The bank that has your account will issue a 1099-SA showing all the money you took out of the account, and the IRS has a right to audit to see whether the expenses are legitimate. If they are not, you will be required to pay tax on the *non-medical distributions*. This account belongs to you, and you are entitled to use the money, even if you no longer work for the employer or have an HDHP. If you are not in an HDHP, are on Medicare or someone else's non-HDHP plan, you may not make contributions. If you pass away while there is still money in your account, it will go to your *beneficiary* (the person who gets your money after you are gone) tax-free if they use the money for qualified medical, prescriptions, dental, or vision expenses. Contact your HR department or go to https://www.irs.gov for the current maximum annual contribution amount. If you contribute more than the maximum, you may be able to roll it over and count it as a contribution for next year (do as soon as possible) or withdraw the excess amount before the due date of your tax return. Otherwise, you may end up paying a 6% excess-contribution penalty tax for each year the excess amount remains in your account.

➢ ***401k contributions*** to a traditional (original type before Roth) retirement account are pre-tax. A 401k retirement plan is a plan your employer sets up with an investment company, designed to help you save for retirement. Maybe this seems like a long way off for most of you reading this book, but use time to your advantage and start saving for retirement as early as possible. Employers can choose to have your 401k plan offer both traditional and Roth retirement accounts. Only contributions made to the traditional 401k are pre-tax. Refer to *You Snooze, You Lose* for more information on retirement plans and the differences between traditional and Roth. Contributions you make to a traditional 401k are deducted from your pay pre-tax.

DID YOU KNOW?

Most employer contributions to your retirement plan go into your traditional retirement account, meaning they are not taxable to you now, but they will be later when you withdraw them. However, the SECURE 2.0 Act of 2022, a federal law enacted to encourage employees to save for retirement, allows employers to give you the option of having your matches go into your traditional or Roth retirement account—employers are not required to give employees a choice and not all plans offer this.

If you choose to have your match put in your traditional account, you will not be taxed now, but you will be taxed when you withdraw the money. If you choose to have your match put into your Roth account, you will be taxed now through your payroll tax deductions.

Post-Tax Benefits

Now that we have talked about some of the more common pre-tax benefits, let's talk about a couple of post-tax benefits.

- ➢ ***Insurance benefits*** may be post-tax. Always ask your human resources department as benefits vary from company to company.
- ➢ ***Roth 401k contributions*** are post-tax. A Roth account may or may not be included in your 401k plan. Employers choose whether to offer Roth. Like a traditional 401k account, your contributions will come out of your pay, but unlike a traditional account, they will not be deducted before calculating your taxes. Because you are paying the taxes now, you will not owe any taxes in the future when you withdraw the money. Your growth in a Roth account is also never taxed. Since Roth and traditional accounts are handled differently for taxes, the money for these accounts always has to be kept separate. It may look like one account, but the money is segregated by Roth and traditional. Some employers' plans offer free financial advice from a licensed financial advisor. If the balance of your Roth passes to a beneficiary, they will not pay any taxes on the money either, if the Roth account was opened at least five years prior. Refer to *You*

Snooze, You Lose for more about the differences between a traditional 401k account and a Roth.

Employer Paid Benefits

There are also some benefits that may be free to you.

- ➤ *Life Insurance* policy premiums are sometimes paid by the employer. If the face value—the amount that will be paid to the beneficiary—of the life insurance does not exceed $50,000 of life insurance coverage, you incur no tax on this benefit.
- ➤ *Short-term and Long-term disability insurance* is sometimes paid in full by the employer; there is no cost or tax required from you. If you receive disability payments, however, you will be taxed on the amount of money you receive.
- ➤ *Tuition reimbursement* is sometimes offered by the employer, and a portion of the reimbursement may be taxable. The IRS sets limits on how much an employer can pay before you are taxed. In 2025, the limit is $5,250, so if your employer reimbursed you $7,000, you would be taxed on $1,750 (7,000-5,250).

Other Deductions

In addition to benefits, you may have other deductions such as *union dues* (a fee charged to belong to a union), *garnishments* (a court-ordered amount withheld from your pay to satisfy a debt), and *donations* (money collected for a charity drive). These are all post-tax deductions.

13

Taxes on Earned Income

Regardless of your age, if you have income from a job, you may be required to file a tax return and pay income taxes. After you have been hired, you will be given paperwork to complete, some of which is your tax information. Because state and local taxes vary, this discussion will only focus on federal taxes, although you will be required to complete paperwork for your state and local taxes too. To calculate your federal taxes, you will be given a W-4 form. See Figure 13.1 IRS Form W-4.

Your employer will use the information you provide on your W-4 form to calculate the federal income tax amount to be withheld from your pay. To complete your W-4 form, you enter your name, address, social security number, and your filing status (such as Single, Married Filing Jointly, or Head of Household). In Step 2, you enter information only if you work multiple jobs or your spouse works too. Step 3 asks for the number of dependents, usually the number of people in your household that you are responsible for supporting such as you, your spouse, and your dependent children. Be sure to enter the number of qualifying children under age seventeen on the line indicated because they have a different deduction amount than your other dependents. *Note: each person can only be claimed by one person. Therefore, if you live with your parents and your parents claim you as a dependent, you will not be entitled to claim yourself too.*

Other credits refers to other tax credits you expect to have when you file, such as Earned Income Credit, Adoption Credit, or Lifetime Learning Credit.

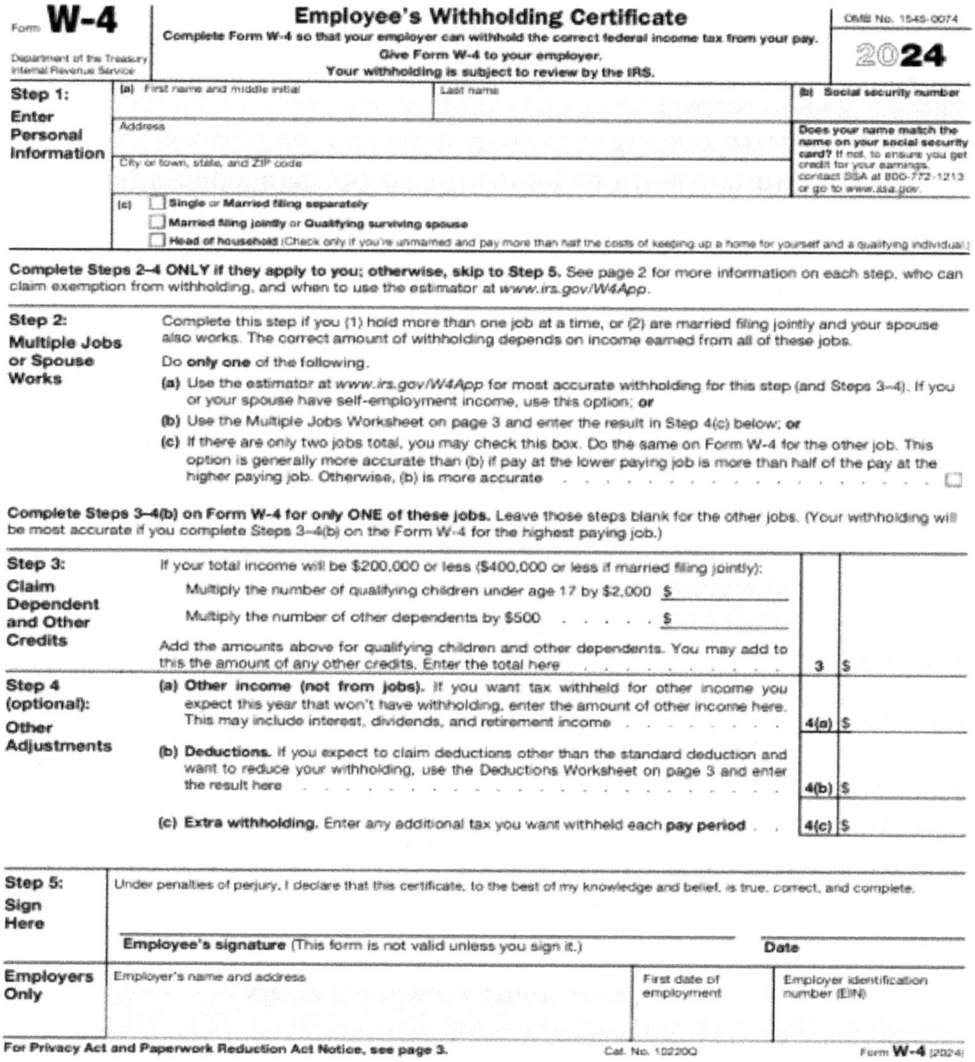

Form **W-4**

Department of the Treasury
Internal Revenue Service

Employee's Withholding Certificate

Complete Form W-4 so that your employer can withhold the correct federal income tax from your pay.
Give Form W-4 to your employer.
Your withholding is subject to review by the IRS.

OMB No. 1545-0074

2024

Step 1: Enter Personal Information

(a) First name and middle initial | Last name | (b) Social security number

Address

City or town, state, and ZIP code

Does your name match the name on your social security card? If not, to ensure you get credit for your earnings, contact SSA at 800-772-1213 or go to www.ssa.gov.

(c) ☐ **Single** or **Married filing separately**
☐ **Married filing jointly** or **Qualifying surviving spouse**
☐ **Head of household** (Check only if you're unmarried and pay more than half the costs of keeping up a home for yourself and a qualifying individual.)

Complete Steps 2–4 ONLY if they apply to you; otherwise, skip to Step 5. See page 2 for more information on each step, who can claim exemption from withholding, and when to use the estimator at *www.irs.gov/W4App*.

Step 2: Multiple Jobs or Spouse Works

Complete this step if you (1) hold more than one job at a time, or (2) are married filing jointly and your spouse also works. The correct amount of withholding depends on income earned from all of these jobs.

Do **only one** of the following.

(a) Use the estimator at *www.irs.gov/W4App* for most accurate withholding for this step (and Steps 3–4). If you or your spouse have self-employment income, use this option; **or**

(b) Use the Multiple Jobs Worksheet on page 3 and enter the result in Step 4(c) below; **or**

(c) If there are only two jobs total, you may check this box. Do the same on Form W-4 for the other job. This option is generally more accurate than (b) if pay at the lower paying job is more than half of the pay at the higher paying job. Otherwise, (b) is more accurate . . . . ☐

Complete Steps 3–4(b) on Form W-4 for only ONE of these jobs. Leave those steps blank for the other jobs. (Your withholding will be most accurate if you complete Steps 3–4(b) on the Form W-4 for the highest paying job.)

Step 3: Claim Dependent and Other Credits

If your total income will be $200,000 or less ($400,000 or less if married filing jointly):

Multiply the number of qualifying children under age 17 by $2,000 $

Multiply the number of other dependents by $500 . . . . . $

Add the amounts above for qualifying children and other dependents. You may add to this the amount of any other credits. Enter the total here . . . . **3** $

Step 4 (optional): Other Adjustments

(a) Other income (not from jobs). If you want tax withheld for other income you expect this year that won't have withholding, enter the amount of other income here. This may include interest, dividends, and retirement income . . . . **4(a)** $

(b) Deductions. If you expect to claim deductions other than the standard deduction and want to reduce your withholding, use the Deductions Worksheet on page 3 and enter the result here . . . . **4(b)** $

(c) Extra withholding. Enter any additional tax you want withheld each **pay period** . . **4(c)** $

Step 5: Sign Here

Under penalties of perjury, I declare that this certificate, to the best of my knowledge and belief, is true, correct, and complete.

Employee's signature (This form is not valid unless you sign it.) | **Date**

Employers Only

Employer's name and address | First date of employment | Employer identification number (EIN)

For Privacy Act and Paperwork Reduction Act Notice, see page 3. Cat. No. 10220Q Form **W-4** (2024)

FIGURE 13.1 IRS FORM W-4

Step 4 allows you to add other income that you will owe taxes on so the estimated taxes can be deducted from your pay. The deduction section is where you can enter additional deductions you will have over the standard amount (such as itemizing deductions). You can also enter an additional dollar amount you want your employer to withhold from your pay for federal taxes. The amount of income taxable for federal income tax is your gross income minus pretax items that are deducted from your income before your federal taxes are calculated. Refer to the example of pay, benefits, and taxes. Your W-4 form can be changed at any time by completing a new form and turning it into your human resources or payroll department.

In addition to federal income tax, you will also be taxed for the Federal Insurance Contributions Act (FICA), which is comprised of two types of tax—social security tax and medicare tax. Currently the tax rate for the social security portion is 6.2% and the portion for medicare is 1.45%, for a total FICA tax of 7.65%. Employers are also required to pay their share of the social security and medicare amounts which are the same amounts you pay through your tax withholdings (amounts deducted from your pay). They must include their share when they remit (pay) your taxes. *Some pretax benefits are taxable for social security and medicare even though they are not taxed for federal income tax.* An example would be a 401k contribution. Refer to Figure 13.2 Example of Pay, Benefits, and Taxes.

The illustration below is based on the following and shows how the taxes are calculated:

Hourly pay rate is 12.50 per hour; worked 40 hours.

Gross Pay (12.50 * 40) $500

Federal income tax rate is 15%

Employee share of pre-tax health insurance $20

Employee regular 401k contribution $30

Employee Roth 401k contribution $25

TAXES ON EARNED INCOME

	PAY AND WITHHOLDINGS	TAXABLE INCOME FOR FEDERAL INCOME TAX	TAXBLE INCOME FOR SOCIAL SECURITY AND MEDICARE
Gross Pay	500.00	500.00	500.00
Pre-tax health insurance	(20.00)	(20.00)	(20.00)
Regular 401k	(30.00)	(30.00)	0
Roth 401k	(25.00)	0	0
Pay before Taxes	425.00		
Taxable Income		450.00	480.00
Taxes Withheld	(104.22)	67.50	36.72
Net Pay	320.78		

Figure 13.2 Example of Pay, Benefits, and Taxes

Pre-tax health insurance is not taxable at all, so $20 is deducted from gross pay when calculating federal income taxes and FICA. Regular 401k contributions are not taxable for federal income tax purposes, but are subject to social security and medicare. Therefore, $30 is only deducted from gross pay for federal income tax. Roth 401k contributions are fully taxable so they are not deducted at all. The illustration shows that our taxable income for Federal Income Tax is $450 and the tax is $67.50 ($450 * 15% tax rate). The taxable income for FICA tax is $480 and the FICA tax is $36.72 ($480 * 7.65%). Taxes withheld can differ from your total tax on your return based on your filing status and other deductions. See tax tables for the current year at https://www.irs.gov.

With hourly or salaried employment, your employer will withhold your taxes and remit to the proper tax authority on your behalf. The one exception may be your local taxes. In many states, employers are not required to withhold local taxes for where you live if different from where you work. Many employers will withhold and pay the local taxes for you as a courtesy, but if yours does not, you are still responsible for paying your local taxes. Your local tax authority may also require you to make quarterly payments if your employer is not withholding. Some local tax districts have reciprocal agreements with each other, and you may get a discount if you must pay two local tax authorities, such as where you work and where you live. Ask your human resources department if you are unsure about local taxes. If you live in one state and work in another, work in more than one state, or moved to another state during the year, you will need to file state tax returns in both states. Different states have different tax rules, so be sure to get professional help if this applies to you.

If you work more than one job, you may need to ask your employers to take out more for taxes.

Taxes are charged based on income levels and the tax return filing status you entered on your W-4: single, married filing separately, married filing jointly, qualifying surviving spouse, or head of household. The tax brackets for 2024 for Single filing status are shown in Figure 13.3 Example of Tax Brackets. Each tax bracket is for a different level of income. The higher the income, the higher the tax rate.

2024 FEDERAL INCOME TAX BRACKETS FILING STATUS: SINGLE		
TAX RATE	TAXABLE INCOME	
	FROM	TO
10%	$0	$11,600
12%	$11,601	$47,150
22%	$47,151	$100,525

Figure 13.3 Example of Tax Brackets

As you can see, Figure 13.3 shows that if I made $65,000, my income would be split and taxed at different rates. The first $11,600 of my income would be taxed at 10%, the second part $35,550 ($47,150-11,600) would be taxed at 12%, and the third part $17,850 ($65,000-47,150) would be taxed at 22%. Refer to Figure 13.4 Example of How You May Owe Taxes if You Work Multiple Jobs.

TAXES ON EARNED INCOME

TWO SEPARATE EMPLOYERS WITHHOLDING TAX				COMBINED INCOME AND TAX FOR TAX RETURN			
	TAX RATE	WAGES	TAX		TAX RATE	WAGES	TAX
	10%	11,600	1,160		10%	11,600	1,160
	12%	33,400	4,008		12%	35,550	4,266
EMPLOYER #1	TOTAL	45,000	5,168		22%	17,850	3,927
				COMBINED TOTALS		65,000	9,353
	TAX RATE	WAGES	TAX	AMOUNT WITHHELD FROM PAY			7,336
	10%	11,600	1,160				
	12%	8,400	1,008	TAX DUE WITH TAX RETURN			2,017
EMPLOYER #2	TOTAL	20,000	2,168				
TOTALS PER PAY		65,000	7,336				

Figure 13.4 Example of How You May Owe Taxes if You Work Multiple Jobs

Because there are different tax rates for different income levels, working more than one job can sometimes cause you to owe taxes. So, let's look at how working two jobs can sometimes bump you into a higher tax bracket. Imagine you have two jobs and you make $45,000 at one and $20,000 at the other, for a total income of $65,000. Each employer will base the taxes they withhold only on the amount you make at their workplace according to the current tax brackets (unless you indicated on your W-4 form that you work two jobs).

Note that your income from Employer #1 ($45,000) does not exceed the first two tax brackets, and the income from Employer #2 ($20,000) does not exceed the first two tax brackets. However, when you combine the income for your tax return, you can see that $65,000 does exceed the first two tax brackets and part of the income is taxed at 22%. Your income from two employers when added together bumped you up to the next income tax bracket of 22%. Therefore, *if you work more than one job, you may need to ask your employers to take out more for taxes by completing a new W-4 form.*

Employees Year-end Tax Form W-2

All employees will receive a W-2—with copies to file with their tax returns—from their employer by January 31st of the following year (or the next business day if the 31st falls on a weekend). This will provide the information needed to file their taxes. A copy of the W-2 will also be sent to tax authorities, and employees are required to attach a copy to each tax return. If they are filing their taxes electronically, they will need to enter the information. The W-2 will show their gross taxable pay for each type of tax, the tax paid on their behalf, and other information, such as their contributions to their retirement plan, and employer contributions to their health savings plan. Employees should review this for accuracy and immediately report any errors to human resources to get a corrected W-2. To verify accuracy, the W-2 information can be compared to the year to date information on the last pay stub of the year. Refer to Figure 13.5 Sample W-2.

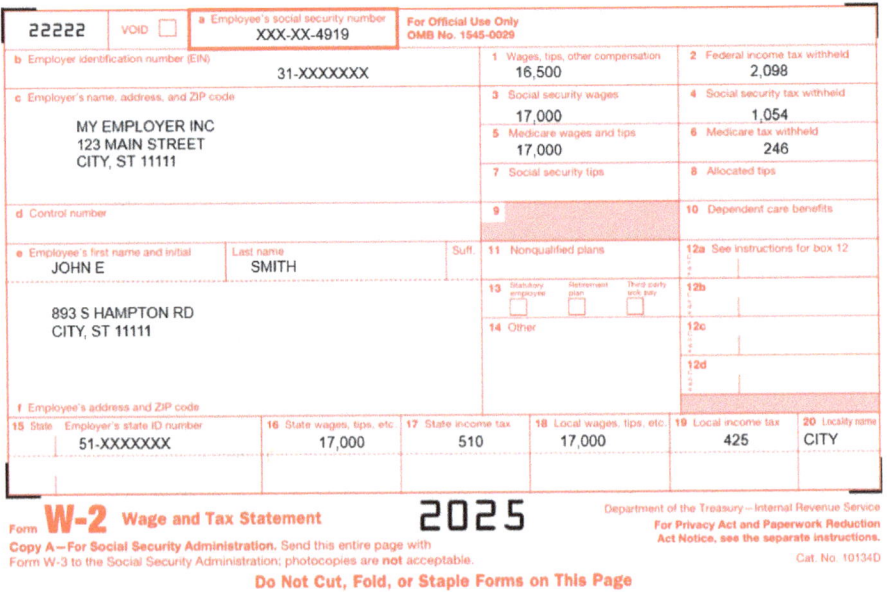

Figure 13.5 Sample W-2

If you are a contractor, and therefore self-employed, you will not receive a W-2. Contractors will receive a Form 1099 NEC (for non-employee compensation) at the end of the year from the individuals or businesses for whom they worked. It will show the total that was paid during the year. As a contractor, you need to keep records of all your contract income, as well as the amount of taxes you have paid. A 1099 NEC will only show *the amount of income you received* from that individual or business. It will not show the amount of taxes you paid. If you worked for multiple individuals or businesses during the year, you will receive multiple 1099s. The IRS does not require individuals or businesses to send out 1099s for amounts under $600, *but you are still required to report all income and pay taxes owed.*

As long as you pay in (through payroll taxes or estimated taxes) at least 90% of this year's total tax (the total amount, not the amount due) or 100% of last year's total tax, you will not be assessed an underpayment penalty. You must still pay any additional amount due for this year by the deadline for filing your taxes.

You may need to make quarterly estimated tax payments to the appropriate tax authorities by the due date. If you also have W-2 wages, and you have your employer take out enough taxes from your pay to cover the taxes you owe for your 1099 NEC income (income received as a contractor), then you may not need to make quarterly payments. However, if no taxes are paid on your behalf during the year, you may be assessed with penalties and interest. As long as you pay in (through payroll taxes and/or estimated taxes) at least 90% of this year's total tax (the total amount, not the amount due) or 100% of last year's total tax, you will not be assessed an underpayment penalty. You must still pay any additional amount due for this year by the deadline for filing your taxes. Refer to Figure 13.6 Sample Year End Tax Form 1099 NEC (for Contractors).

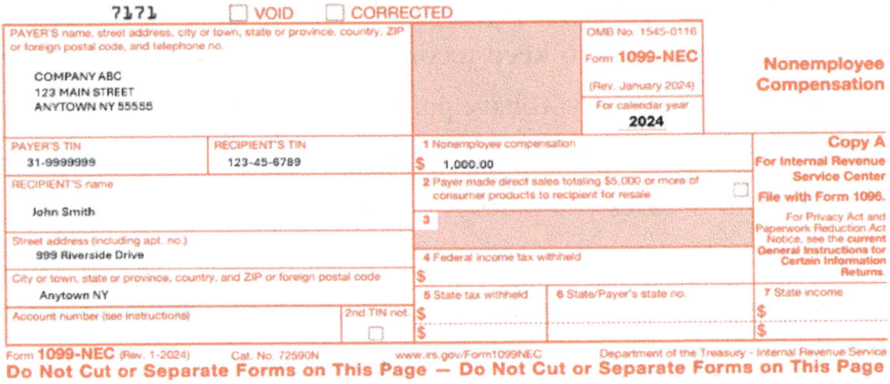

7171 VOID CORRECTED

PAYER'S name, street address, city or town, state or province, country, ZIP or foreign postal code, and telephone no.
COMPANY ABC
123 MAIN STREET
ANYTOWN NY 55555

OMB No. 1545-0116
Form 1099-NEC
(Rev. January 2024)
For calendar year 2024

Nonemployee Compensation

PAYER'S TIN: 31-9999999
RECIPIENT'S TIN: 123-45-6789

1 Nonemployee compensation: $ 1,000.00

Copy A
For Internal Revenue Service Center
File with Form 1096.

RECIPIENT'S name: John Smith

2 Payer made direct sales totaling $5,000 or more of consumer products to recipient for resale

3

For Privacy Act and Paperwork Reduction Act Notice, see the current General Instructions for Certain Information Returns.

Street address (including apt. no.): 999 Riverside Drive

4 Federal income tax withheld: $

City or town, state or province, country, and ZIP or foreign postal code: Anytown NY

5 State tax withheld: $ / $
6 State/Payer's state no.
7 State income: $ / $

Account number (see instructions)
2nd TIN not.

Form 1099-NEC (Rev. 1-2024) Cat. No. 72590N www.irs.gov/Form1099NEC Department of the Treasury - Internal Revenue Service
Do Not Cut or Separate Forms on This Page — Do Not Cut or Separate Forms on This Page

Figure 13.6 Sample Year End Tax Form 1099-NEC (For Contractors)

The current tax law states if you make more than $400 in 1099 NEC income (pay for work as a contractor), you must also pay self-employment taxes, which are currently 15.3%. This tax covers the social security and medicare taxes for what the employee would normally have withheld from their pay (7.65%) plus the employer's amount since you are self-employed (7.65%). Refer to the section on *Payroll Taxes* for more information. Self-employment taxes are federal taxes and can be paid with your federal income tax. In addition, you may also have state and local taxes you need to pay. Therefore, if you make more than $400 as a contractor you should plan to save money aside to cover what you will owe in taxes. The amount of tax you will owe will vary depending on how much, if any, you have withheld on W-2 income, your filing status, dependents, and level of income. To make estimated tax payments to the federal government online, you can go to https://directpay.irs.gov, select *Make Payment.* If the tax ID of your business is not your social security number, you need to go to https://www.eftps.gov/eftps/ to make payments online. You can still mail in a payment along with a 1040-ES coupon (form) instead of paying online if you prefer.

With 1099 NEC income, you are considered self-employed and will need to file a Schedule C Profit or Loss from Business with your 1040 Federal Income Tax return. You will report your income and related business expenses on form Schedule C—income taxes and self-employment taxes are not considered a business expense and are not to be deducted on your Schedule C. Your self-employment taxes are reported on Schedule SE Self-Employment Taxes and will also be filed with your federal income tax return. You are entitled to pay into a traditional or Roth IRA, and any traditional contributions you make may be deducted on your tax return Form 1040. Retirement contributions are not to be deducted on your Schedule C. For more details go to https://www.irs.gov and search for 1040, Schedule C. There are other types of businesses that may get 1099s, but since we are focusing on contractor's income, we will not cover those topics. Refer to Figure 13.7 Page 1 of Form 1040 Schedule C Profit or Loss from Business.

Figure 13.7 Page 1 of Form 1040 Schedule C Profit or Loss From Business

If you decide to start a business, I recommend you get some professional advice. States have their own rules for setting up a business, and federal tax laws vary depending on the type of business structure.

DEEPER DIVE

There are many types of business structures. Below is a list of several of the more common types of for-profit businesses.

Sole Proprietor: an unincorporated business with one owner. There is no legal separation between the company and the owner. This is the easiest to establish and is popular for small businesses, individual contractors, and consultants.

Partnership: a formal arrangement between two or more parties to manage and operate a business. It also describes how the profits will be shared. There are three main types of partnerships: General, Limited, and Limited Liability.

S Corp: a for-profit corporation. It is only available for businesses with one hundred or fewer owners. The primary difference between an S Corp and a C Corp is its taxation. An S Corp may pass through business profits/losses, deductions, and credits directly to its shareholders without paying any federal corporate tax, also known as a pass-through entity.

Limited Liability Company (LLC): a corporation which protects its owners' personal assets in the case that the business gets sued.

It can elect to be a pass-through entity like the S Corp, or it may choose to be taxed like a C Corp.

C Corp: a for-profit business which has its own taxes separate from the owners.

#4 I WORK HARD FOR THE MONEY

ACROSS:

1. Income earned before withholdings for benefits or taxes
3. This type of work is based on an agreement between two parties—there are no benefits and taxes are not withheld
5. This type of 401k contribution is a pre-tax benefit and reduces your income taxes
8. HSA stands for this pre-tax benefit (3 words)
10. These salaried employees do not get overtime pay
12. Salaried employees that are entitled to overtime pay
13. This type of 401k contribution is a post-tax benefit meaning it does not reduce your taxes
15. This type of benefit reduces your income taxes
16. This type of employee usually gets paid the same amount each pay period

DOWN:

2. Where contractors report their 1099 NEC income on their federal tax return
4. The difference between gross income and net income
6. The type of income you have to work for
7. This type of employee gets paid for the amount of time spent working
9. This pay is also called take home pay (2 words)
11. This type of worker gets a W-2 form showing their total earnings and taxes for the year
14. Medicare and social security taxes are what type of taxes?

14

Money That Works Hard for Me

Passive Income

Now that we have covered earned income, let's talk about passive income. Earlier, we said that money doesn't do anything until we choose to do something with it. Making good decisions about what to do with your money can allow your money to grow. Passive income is money you receive *without* working for it—people or institutions pay you for the use of your money or something you own.

SUM IT UP

Common Types of Passive Income:

Interest and Dividends is the money received from savings and investments.

Rental income is the money received for leasing property you own.

Residual income is money received from distribution of content, such as an actor earning money every time the content is shown.

Royalty income is the money received for something like a patent on an invention.

Royalty interest is money received for mineral rights, such as oil and gas production on property you own.

Capital Gain is money received by selling an asset, such as a stock, at a profit (sold for more than the cost).

Not all passive income is taxed at your regular income tax rate (some can be lower), and it is not subject to social security and medicare taxes. Therefore, passive income is the preferred type of income because you do not have to work to get it and you pay less taxes on passive income, so you get to keep more of it.

Robert T. Kiyosaki created games called *CASHFLOW*™ 101 and *CASHFLOW*™ 202 to help you improve your financial skills. Even though these are older games, they are still relevant today. In *CASHFLOW*™ 101 the goal is to get out of the *rat race*—the unpleasant life of people who have jobs that require them to work very hard to compete with others for money, power, status, etc. To get out of the rat race, your passive income must be enough to pay your bills/expenses. *CASHFLOW*™ 101 is a fun game to play and helps you understand how to improve your financial situation. You can also access this game for free on his website, https://www.richdad.com.

Kiyosaki also has a number of good books, such as *Rich Dad, Poor Dad*, *Cash Flow Quadrant*, and *Rich Kid, Poor Kid*. While these books have a lot of valuable information, I offer a word of caution on his views of using other people's money to grow wealth. This requires going into debt, which has inherent risk. I do not advise going into debt to build wealth. Sectors, such as real estate, have ups and downs, and if you are in a lot of debt during a downturn, you can really hurt, if not ruin, your finances. I agree with him that we all need to learn about things we may not necessarily like, such as taxes and finances, because they affect us. However, I do not share his opinion about foregoing doing what we love to achieve great financial wealth. Happiness in life is not only attained through money. If you enjoy what you do, feel a sense of purpose in your life, and make wise financial choices that lead to financial stability, your life will be rich in happiness even without a vast amount of wealth.

We mentioned several types of passive income. It's good to have money coming in from more than one source, because if one source dries up, you will have another. Robert G. Allen has written a couple of good books about how to create different sources of income. If you are interested in learning how to create passive income, you can read more about it through his books, *Multiple Streams of Income,* and *Multiple Streams of Internet Income.* He can also be found on YouTube, X (BestSellerBob), and Instagram (Nothingdownrobertallen).

The best way to increase your passive income is to save, invest more, and spend less. The more money you put to work, the more money it will generate. When you get a raise at work, don't go out and buy a bigger home, car, or other expensive things. Unless you have a true need to get a bigger home or car, continue living the way you did before the raise. People who buy bigger and better (spend) every time they get a raise are not making decisions that will move them toward financial independence. When you save and invest, your money makes more money, and eventually you may have enough passive income to pay your bills. Then you will no longer have to work to support yourself. Refer to the section on *Passive Income* for more information.

15

Where to Grow Money

To save and invest, you will need to open an account if you do not already have one. If you are a U.S. citizen, eighteen years or older, you will need to provide your social security number, a valid government ID such as a driver's license, passport, state, or military ID, and money to deposit. If you are under eighteen, you will need a parent or guardian to go with you and sign for the account. The primary accounts found at a bank, credit union, or savings and loan are: checking, savings, money market, and certificates of deposit (CD). Some bank accounts have fees or require you to maintain a minimum balance. Some pay interest and some, such as a certificate of deposit, need to be kept in the account until maturity (reaches the due date) or you will lose interest. All these requirements should be stated up front by the financial institution. If they do not tell you, or you do not find where it is written on the paperwork, be sure to ask.

Checking accounts do not pay interest to you, but may charge a bank fee. These accounts may come with starter checks and a debit card. Although fewer people use paper checks today, you should still understand how they are used. A paper check is an I.O.U. You complete the check for the amount you owe along with the person's name after "Pay to the order of" and sign it. Your signature gives the bank permission to pay the person with money from your bank account. They can take the check to a bank and get cash or have the money deposited into their own account. Once they cash the check, the money will come out of your account. See Figure 15.1 Example of a Check.

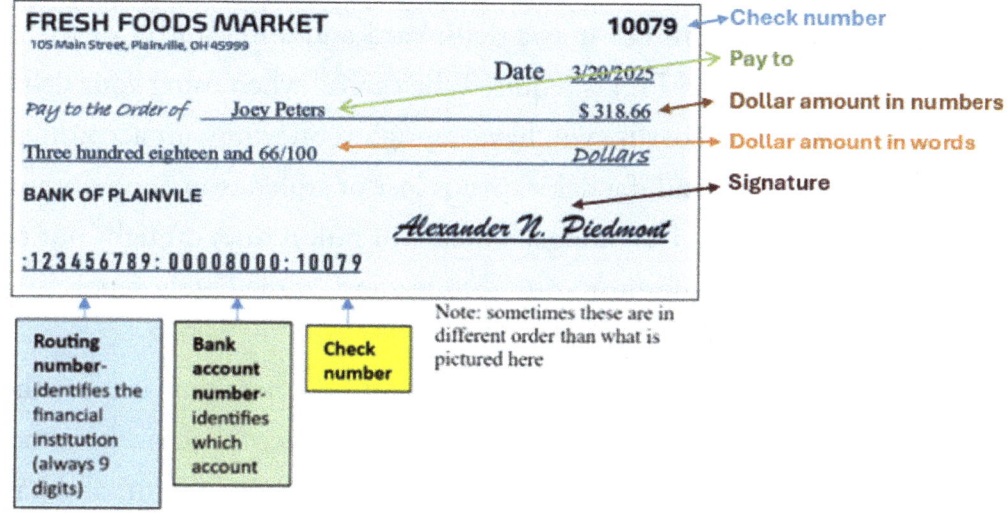

Figure 15.1 Example of a Check

If someone gives you money in the form of a check, you need to sign your name on the back of the check where it says Endorse Here. By signing, you are saying you understand if the check is bad—the person does not have enough money in their checking account to pay the amount on the check—the money will be taken back out of your account. Some banks will charge you a fee if you deposit a check that bounces.

If a debit card is lost or stolen, someone can use it like a credit card and buy things which will pull money straight out of your account. Always monitor your account.

You may also be offered a debit card. A debit card is used like a credit card, but the money comes immediately out of your bank account. Debit cards can also be used at ATMs to withdraw money or deposit checks that you receive. Your bank will give you a PIN (usually a 4-digit number) to access your account. The PIN is a way to prove that it is you. Some ATMs charge a fee so make sure you know which ATMs you can use for free. When you make purchases, you can use it as a debit card and enter a PIN or use it like a credit card, and no PIN is required. Be careful when using your debit card as you need to make sure you have enough money in your account to cover your spending. And if a debit card is lost or stolen, someone can use it like a credit card and buy things, which will pull money straight out of your account. Always monitor your account and immediately report any charges you didn't make to your bank.

It is important to monitor your bank account statement to make sure the charges are legitimate. Banks will tell you how to access your account online. You can review your account, transfer money to another account, and pay bills online. I recommend setting up alerts, so you get a text when money has come out of your account. This is just an extra precaution so you know right away and can determine if the withdrawal is legitimate. Also most banks allow you to take a picture of a check with your phone and deposit it into your account rather than taking it in person. Many employers also allow you to set up your pay to automatically go into your bank account (called direct deposit), so you do not even have to sign and deposit a check.

DEEPER DIVE

When a bank says they are going to credit your account, they mean they are going to add money to your account. This can be confusing because when you add money to your account it is a positive number (or a debit). The bank is talking about their books. When they add money to your account it is a credit for the bank because the bank owes you that money.

Most bank accounts today also have an app such as Zelle for your phone. This allows you to send and receive money. There are also other money apps, such as Apple Pay, PayPal, Venmo, or CashApp. These are ways to send and receive money electronically on the spot. These apps will link to your bank account or credit card. You can find information online about how to set up apps to transfer money. Just make sure the app uses bank protocols to keep your money safe.

If you have a problem spending too much money, it would be wise to avoid apps that make it easy to spend. If you install banking apps on your phone, make sure you have adequate protection on your phone so no one can gain easy access to your bank accounts if your phone is lost or stolen. Be careful using public Wi-Fi too. If you are conducting financial business on a device in public, be sure to set up a Virtual Private Network (VPN) to keep your data secure.

If you are interested in investing in the stock market, you can open an investment account where you can invest in stocks, ETFs, mutual funds, etc. In earlier times, you had to go through a stockbroker to invest in the stock market. Now, you can open a *trading account* and invest on your own online. Trading is the term used for buying and selling stocks. Many companies offer trades with no commission (fee charged for the trade) and have educational courses you can take for free. There are a number of companies such as Charles Schwab, E-Trade, Robinhood, and many more that offer online investment accounts. You can do an internet search to compare the different options. You can also link your trading account to your bank to move money from one account to another.

SUM IT UP

Types of Financial Instruments
Banks and Credit Unions

- Checking
- Savings
- Certificates of Deposit
- Money Markets

Stockbrokers (including online brokerage firms)

- Exchange Traded Funds (ETF's)
- Mutual Funds
- Stocks
- Bonds
- Certificates of Deposit
- Money Markets

16

Formula to Make Money Grow

Compound interest is the eighth wonder of the world. He who understands it, earns it; he who doesn't, pays it.

—ALBERT EINSTEIN, Theoretical Physicist.

We discussed the different types of accounts you can set up so your money can grow. Now let's look at how that happens. Would you rather have $20 or start with a penny and double the value every day for thirty days? It turns out, when you start with a penny and double the previous amount every day for thirty days, you end up with $5,368,709.12. This gives you an idea of how compounding works, as well as how much mere pennies can add up.

One remarkable thing about saving and investing is *compound interest*. Compound interest means that you are getting paid interest on the interest you have already received. Figure 16.1 is based on starting with $5,000 and investing it for five years, earning 5% interest compounded monthly. At the end of five years, you would have $6,416.79, earning $1,416.79 from your original investment.

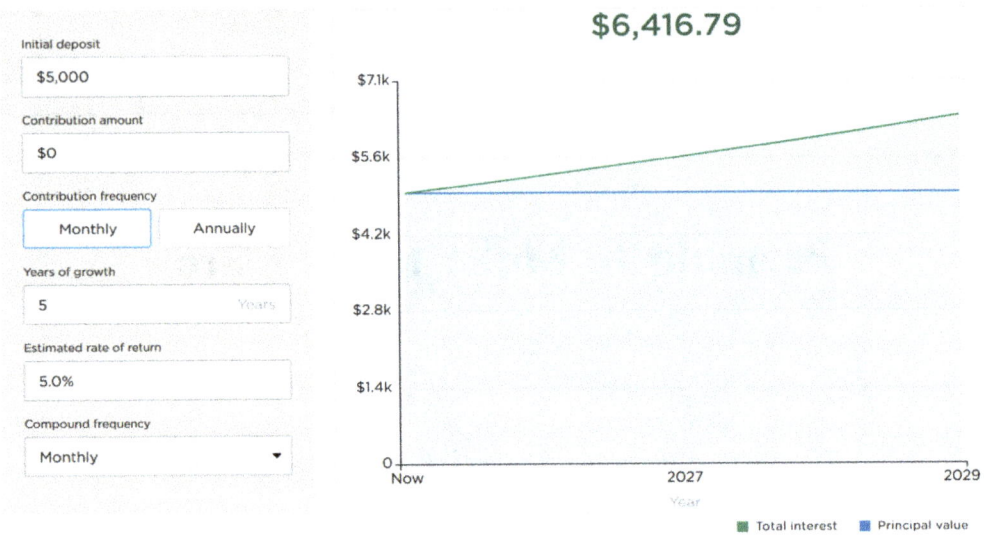

Figure 16.1 Compound Interest from Nerdwallet.com

If you add money each month, you will start to see your savings grow even more. By saving $100 each month, you will add $6,000 over five years, making your total investment $11,000, and your money will have made $2,217.40. See Figure 16.2.

Figure 16.2 Compound Interest from Nerdwallet.com

If you invest more money up front or early, you get more money out of the compounding. In Figure 16.3, the same amount of money was invested, $11,000, but this time the whole amount was invested in the beginning. As you can see in Figure 16.3, the difference at the end of five years is an additional $899.55 in interest and the total interest earned was $3,116.95. The value of your account after five years would be $14,116.95. Remember the doubling of a penny each day for a month and the latte factor®? Saving a little can grow to a lot.

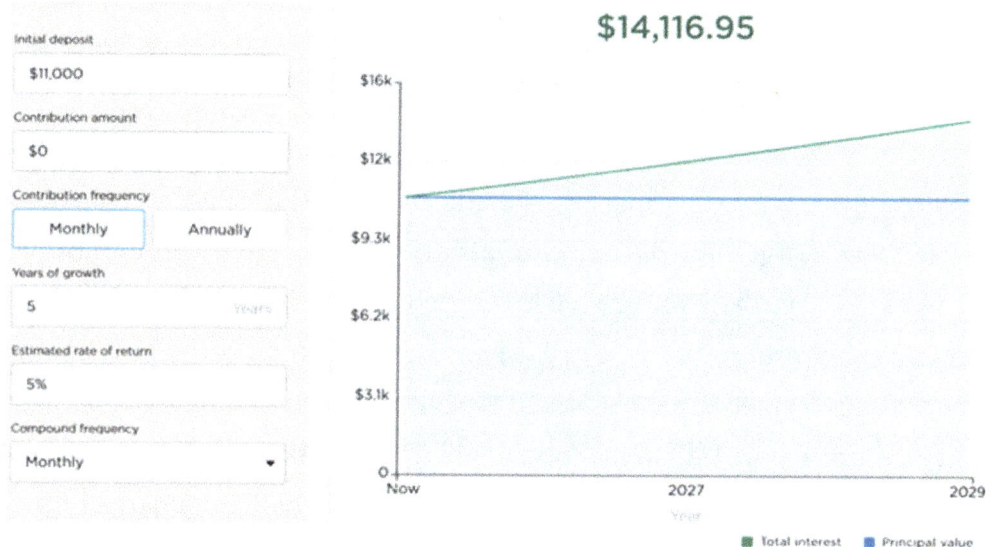

Figure 16.3 Compound Interest from Nerdwallet.com

The previous examples represent how savings accounts, certificates of deposit, and money markets can all grow over time. They are each a little different and can grow at different rates based on the amount of money you put in, the interest rate, and how frequently the interest compounds. Let's look at each type of account. A *savings account* typically pays the lowest interest of the three, and there is no requirement to keep your money deposited for a certain period, although some require you maintain a minimum balance. Some savings accounts pay more based on how high your balance is. Putting money in a savings account is a great way to start saving.

Certificates of Deposit pay a designated interest rate for a set period, on a certain amount of money. Common CD options may be for one-year, two-year, or three-year, although there are some shorter and some longer. The longer the CD period, the higher the interest, if banks anticipate that interest rates will go up. If banks anticipate interest rates will go down, you may see the longer term has the lower rate. Many people like to ladder CD's, meaning they buy one-year, two-year, and three-year CD's. When the one year comes due, they take that money and put it in a three-year CD, so they continue to have a one-year, two-year, and three-year CD. If you pull your money out early, there can be a financial penalty, meaning you will not get the full amount of interest.

If you really need the money, you can take out a CD loan. It is considered a *secured personal loan* because your certificate of deposit is used as *collateral*. The interest charged for the loan is typically low because if you do not pay, the bank will get their money back from your CD. I opened a CD for my son and let him borrow from it. I asked the bank to report it to the credit bureaus so as he paid it back it would establish a credit history for him. Most banks do not report CD loans so you will have to ask them if they will. He continued to earn the CD rate on his money and the bank charged him a rate close to his rate of return. His loan netted to about a 1% interest rate.

A *money market* is another type of account which is similar to a savings account, but usually requires a larger minimum deposit. Money markets normally pay higher interest and may charge a fee if you go over a certain number of transactions per month. It is a little bit riskier because it is invested in fixed income securities. Those risks are *interest rate risk*—an interest rate change that could negatively affect the investment, *liquidity risk*—the possibility that the financial institution might be unable to meet its obligations, and *credit risk*—the possibility that a borrower may not be able to repay their loan. The safest money market funds are US Treasuries. In recent years, some money market funds offered in retirement accounts had negative returns, so we didn't recommend investing in the money markets at that time. Always do your homework when investing.

DEEPER DIVE

Ever wonder why banks pay you interest? Banks use your money and lend it to people seeking a loan. Let's say Mr. Jones asks the bank to loan him money to buy a house. The bank gets the money from its investors' deposits. The bank may charge Mr. Jones 6% for his mortgage, and pay its depositors 3-5% on their savings and investments. The reason banks pay more for a CD than a regular savings account is because they have a longer timeframe to use the money. This is also why you are penalized on the amount of interest you receive if you pull money out of a long-term investment before it matures. Banks are required to keep a certain amount of money on hand, so it is there when you want to make a withdrawal. The money you have in a bank is also insured by the Federal Deposit Insurance Corporation (FDIC) for up to $250,000 in the case of a bank failure.

You may also have a retirement account at work handled by an investment firm. Some retirement plans allow you to invest in the broad market. Most only allow you to choose from what your company offers in their plan. Employers who offer retirement accounts are required to do a *fiduciary* review of the account at least once per year. A fiduciary is a person or firm legally obligated to act in your best interest. This evaluation is to ensure that you have enough funds to diversify—have a mixture of large, medium, and small cap as well as bonds, fixed income, domestic and international options—the funds offered are doing well, and your investment firm is serving you well at a competitive rate.

A trading account can be either a regular investment account or a retirement account—Roth IRA or regular IRA. There are limits to how much you can invest in an IRA based on your income. The most common investments are: *ETFs* (Exchange Traded Funds), *mutual funds*, *stocks*, and *bonds*. ETFs and mutual funds are like a basket of stocks or bonds, meaning the fund pools investors' money and buys shares of stocks or bonds. Many people prefer to buy ETF's or mutual funds instead of individual stocks. It is often less expensive to own shares through a fund than individually, and it helps spread risk because you aren't putting all your eggs in one basket. You can also compare them with other similar investments.

Although ETF's and mutual funds are similar, they trade very differently. ETF's trade like a stock. When you buy or sell shares in an ETF, the trade closes at that time. Mutual funds do not trade like a stock, and it may take a couple of days to find out what the trade price was. There are also rules about how often you can trade mutual funds.

Offerings—issues or sales of a security—made on the stock markets are required by the *SEC* (Securities and Exchange Commission) to file a prospectus, which gives details about their operations for potential investors. When investing, always look at the *prospectus*, *expense ratios*—what expense percentage is charged on the investment, *advisory fees*—fees charged by an advisor, *dividends*—share of the earnings distributed to shareholders, if any, *index*—such as S&P 500, Russell 1000, etc., *investing goals*, *Morningstar rating*—a one to five star rating to help investors see estimated risk and reward for stocks and funds long term, and *historical return*. You can get a lot of information about a company by looking at its profile in the information provided by your trading company. Refer to Figures 16.4 and 16.5. You can also compare funds that have a similar investment strategy to help you decide where to invest.

Figure 16.4 Sample ETF Research Page from Ameritrade (now Charles Schwab)

Figure 16.5 Sample ETF Research page from TD Ameritrade (Now Charles Schwab)

Figure 16.5 is an example of a Profile page from TD Ameritrade. Although different investment companies offer the same information about the investments offered, you will have to look for it. Each company organizes their information differently. The *Performance* tab will show you the stock's or fund's past performance. The *Ratings and Risk* tab will go into more detail about how the fund is rated and what the risk is. The *Portfolio* tab will give a list of what the fund is invested in, such as which stocks and the percentage for each. The Morningstar Style Box on the right shows whether the fund is large, medium, or small cap, which indicates the size of the company. Cap refers to capitalization, or size. It will also tell you how much risk and return you could expect. Below the Morningstar boxes is a list of other ratings by analysts, including whether they think this is a good time to buy, hold, or sell. Note that some of the analysts report on the short term, which is more for day traders, rather than people investing for the long term.

DID YOU KNOW?

Often times, you can see the stock market go up or down as soon as the Federal Reserve makes an announcement, such as they are going to cut interest rates. Many people, especially day traders (people not invested for the long term) quickly react to news from the Federal Reserve because the Fed's actions can be an indicator of the current state of the economy, as well as where the economy may be headed.

Beware that people tend to panic and rush to sell their shares if the stock market goes down. This panic sell off can cause the stock market to go down even more. If you know there is trouble with a certain stock or fund you own and its metrics indicate it is no longer a sound investment, then selling should be a consideration. However, the stock market goes up and down all the time. If you know your investments are solid—meaning the metrics you evaluated when you decided to buy them are still good—do not sell just because the market is down. When a store has a sale, people buy because it is a good deal. If the market goes down, but your stock or fund is still good, this is usually the time to buy more shares, not sell.

If you are adding money on a regular basis, like through your 401k plan, you are dollar cost averaging (DCA). Dollar cost averaging, first coined by Benjamin Graham in his book, *The Intelligent Investor*, means that sometimes you buy at a lower price because the market is down and sometimes you buy at a higher price when the market is up. For example, let's say you get paid each week and you have $100 withheld from your pay that goes into your 401k plan and buys shares of a fund. Last week the fund was trading at $25 per share. That means you were able to buy 4 shares ($100 ÷ $25 = 4). But this week the fund price is $20 per share. That means, this week, you are able to buy 5 shares ($100 ÷ $20 = 5). When the price is lower, you can get more shares for the same amount of money. When the price goes up, your money buys fewer shares, but the value of all of your shares went up. Overall, this strategy means you are probably getting a satisfactory overall price per share for your holdings.

DEEPER DIVE

Dividends on investments can be taken either as cash or used to buy more shares of the investment that issued the dividend. In a dividend reinvestment plan (DRIP), you indicate which investments you want to buy more shares of the stock, mutual fund, or ETF that issued the dividend. Every investment you select will automatically buy more shares for you every time a dividend is issued. This is an excellent way to grow your investments. I highly recommend stocks or funds that pay dividends. A good place to look for investments that pay dividends is the list of Dividend Aristocrats. Companies on this list have a history of paying and increasing dividends.

In a trading account, you can also invest in CDs, money markets, stocks, and bonds. Stocks are what publicly traded companies offer to sell for a share of ownership in their company. To buy or sell individual stocks, you enter how many shares of the stock you want to buy or sell. Investing in the stock market is beyond the focus of this book, so we will not go into more detail here. If you decide to invest in the stock market, do your homework first. There is risk as well as reward. Many companies with trading accounts offer free classes on investing.

You can also go to <u>https://www.stockmarketgame.org</u> which is an online investment simulator created by the Securities Industry and Financial Markets Association (sifma.org) to help people learn about how to invest in the stock market. You can do this alone or with a friend. Minors need to have an adult sign them up. Teachers can sign up their students to use as a tool in the classroom.

The Security Investor Protection Corporation (SIPC) protects against the loss of cash and securities—such as stocks and bonds you have at a brokerage firm. The limit of SIPC protection is $500,000, which includes a $250,000 limit for cash. This *only* insures against losses if the brokerage firm fails; it *does not* insure losses due to market performance or making poor investment choices.

BRAINSTORM:

Have I put my money to work for me?

....
....
....

What accounts do I have that will earn passive income for me?

....
....
....
....
....

Are there other places where I can invest my money so it can grow? Where?

....

....

....

....

How much money do I currently earn on my money? (Interest, dividends, growth, etc.)?

....

....

....

....

How can I save and invest more to get additional passive income and make my money grow faster?

....

....

....

....

#5 MONEY WORKS HARD FOR ME

ACROSS:

1. This method pays interest on the interest you already received, making your money grow faster
3. A basket of stocks often found in retirement plans (2 words)
5. Person of firm legally obligated to act in your best interest
6. This type of card, often included with a checking account, is like a credit card but the amount comes out of your bank account
7. Passive income is not subject to these taxes
9. Money that you do not work for (2 words)
11. When passive income is enough to pay for your living expenses, you have achieved this (2 words)
14. This term means when you are regularly investing, sometimes the price is high and sometimes it is low, so overall you are probably getting a fair price (3 words)

DOWN:

1. A financial instrument that pays higher interest than savings but requires you to leave your money invested for a certain period of time—some people like to ladder these (3 words)
2. Money made selling an asset, such as a stock, for more than it cost to buy it (2 words)
4. A type of account where you can buy and sell stocks online
8. The size of a company
10. This is a way to have the dividends from a stock or fund automatically buy more shares of the stock or fund that issued the dividend
12. This is a rating system used to evaluate funds long term: its ratings are 1-5 stars (2 words)
13. The best way to grow your money (2 words)

17

What is Debt?

Debt is money borrowed that you need to repay. The borrower (debtor) normally signs an agreement with the lender (creditor) agreeing to how much will be borrowed (principal), the interest rate, how the interest will be calculated, how and when the debt will be repaid, plus any additional fees that will be charged by the lender. This agreement should also show the total amount to be repaid—principal and interest. Paying your loans according to the terms will help your credit. Not paying loans or paying them late will hurt your credit. Sometimes it can be difficult to get a loan if you don't have a good credit score or employment history. In this case, a bank may ask for a cosigner. A cosigner is someone who can qualify for the loan and agrees in writing to pay off the loan if the primary borrower does not. If a family member or a friend agrees to give you a personal loan instead of borrowing from a lending institution, be sure everything is documented in writing and the document is signed by both parties and notarized.

DID YOU KNOW?

Cosigning a loan can be risky for the cosigner. If you cosign a loan, you should know you share full and equal responsibility for the repayment of the loan. If the primary borrower doesn't make the required payments on the loan, it can negatively affect your credit score and possibly prevent you from getting a loan if you need one. Lenders are not required to notify a cosigner if a payment is missed, so make sure you request to be notified. It might also be wise to request statements or have access to online account information. If the person you cosign for doesn't make the payments, the bank will come after you—sometimes even before the primary borrower—to pay the loan, and you are legally obligated to do so. And if you do not legally own the property the loan was for, you will be unable to sell it to recoup your losses.

There are two broad categories of debt: secured and unsecured.

Secured Debt

Secured debt is a loan where the borrower has put up collateral to secure the debt. *Collateral* is property the lender may take if the borrower does not pay the debt back according to the original agreement with the lender. For example, if you buy a car and do not pay your car loan, the lender can repossess your car. If you have a mortgage on your house and do not pay, the lender can foreclose on your house, and it would then belong to the lender. For additional tips on car loans and mortgages, refer to the section *Big Ticket Items: Buying and Leasing*. Secured debt typically has less strict credit worthiness requirements and charges less interest than unsecured debt because secured debt is less risky. With secured debt, the lender can sell the collateral and get some of their money back.

Even with secured debt, always be sure you know the terms of your loan. When my former husband and I were buying our first home back in 1980, interest was very high and rising. We were able to get a mortgage with an interest rate of 12%. The condominium association paid part of the interest for us, so for the first year, we paid 8%. The 12% rate was an adjustable rate mortgage (ARM), which meant it could increase the following year. This adjustable rate mortgage didn't have a cap on how high it could go, and the following year, our rate went to 17%! There was no way we could afford to make the payments at that rate. Fortunately, we were required to put 20% down to qualify for the loan. That meant that we owned 20% of our home, and the bank owned 80%. I called the bank and said we couldn't afford the payments at that interest rate, so they lowered our monthly payment and took the difference out of the 20% we owned so we wouldn't lose our home. Adjustable-rate mortgages might have a low introductory rate but can cost much more over time. Before you agree to this type of loan, make sure you know how much and how often it can increase, and if you can afford the payments at the higher rates. Personally, I would advise against this type of loan.

Unsecured Debt

Unsecured debt is a loan where the borrower has no collateral against the loan. These types of loans are riskier and typically require a higher credit score and proof of credit worthiness. They usually have higher interest rates too. Credit cards are an example of unsecured debt.

18

How Do Loans Work?

Remember our discussions on compound interest and how it can make your money grow? Well, compound interest is great when it's growing your investments, but not so great if it's growing your debt. The methods used to calculate interest on loans and credit cards vary and can make a substantial difference in what you actually end up paying. The difference between simple and compound interest is shown in Figures 18.1 and 18.2.

Simple Interest = P x I x n

P=Principal: 10,000   I=Interest rate: 0.05   N=Term of loan: 3 years

Simple Interest =(10,000 x 0.05) x 3= $1,500
Simple Interest = $1,500.00

Figure 18.1 Simple Interest Calculation

$$A = P\left(1 + \frac{r}{n}\right)^{nt}$$

A=Amount of Interest	P=Principal: 10,000	r=interest rate (decimal): 0.05
n=number of times per year interest is calculated: annually (one time per year)	t=time in years: 3 years	

Amount of Interest =10,000 ((1 + .05/1)³ -1)
Amount of Interest = 10,000 (1.157625-1)
Amount of Interest = $1,576.25

Figure 18.2 Compound Interest Calculation

As you can see, the difference between a loan calculated using simple interest and a loan calculated using compound interest for the same principal, interest rate, and term is $76.25. More frequent compounding, a higher loan amount, and a longer borrowing period would yield a much bigger difference.

When making payments on a loan, part of your payment will go toward the loan balance, or *principal* (the actual amount borrowed) and reduces your debt, and part of your payment goes toward the *interest* on the loan, which does not lower your debt. For example, maybe your car payment is $503 per month. In the first month, your payment of $503 will be $433 for principal and $70 for interest. If you pay the amount due on time, next month, your payment of $503 will be $434 for the principal and $69 for interest. Each month, a little more will be applied to principal and a little less applied to interest. To understand how your payments will be applied, you can look at an amortization schedule. Refer to Figure 18.3 to see the breakdown. The lending institution will always apply your payment to the interest first so if you don't have the full amount, the interest portion will be paid and what is left will go toward your principal. Since your interest is calculated on the principal balance, the interest portion will not go down on the next payment. The exception to this rule is when the lender preloads the interest up front, and you pay the same amount of interest each time you make a payment. **Beware of loans with preloaded interest.** They can cost a lot more.

Amortization Schedule

Date	Interest	Principal	Balance
Mar. 2024	$70	$433	$27,567
Apr. 2024	$69	$434	$27,133
May. 2024	$68	$435	$26,697
Jun. 2024	$67	$436	$26,261
Jul. 2024	$66	$437	$25,824
Aug. 2024	$65	$439	$25,385
Sep. 2024	$63	$440	$24,945
Oct. 2024	$62	$441	$24,505

Figure 18.3 Amortization Schedule from Amortization-calc.com

Some lenders will allow you to make extra payments. Your loan agreement will state whether prepayments are permitted. If your loan agreement says prepayments are not permitted, paying extra might result in a prepayment penalty. If prepayments are permitted, making an additional principal payment—in addition to your regular monthly payment—can reduce your principal balance and save you money on the interest charged. Lenders should apply the extra to the principal, and you should see that amount deducted from the principal on your account. Be sure to check and make sure it is applied properly. Some lenders will hold the extra payment and apply it to next month's interest or change the due date of your next payment, so it doesn't reduce your principal. If your loan allows for extra payments, and your lender is not applying them to your principal balance in a timely manner, you can file a complaint with the Consumer Financial Protection Bureau at https://www.consumerfinance.gov/complaint/. *In February 2025, operations at the Consumer Financial Protection Bureau were suspended. According to www.gobankingrates.com, other options are to reach out to your bank, file a complaint with the Better Business Bureau (BBB), contact your State Attorney General's office, file a claim in Small Claims Court, contact the Federal Deposit Insurance Corporation (FDIC), contact the Office of the Comptroller of the Currency (OCC), contact the Federal Reserve, contact the Federal Trade Commission, or contact your State Banking Agency. For credit unions, you may contact The National Credit Union Administration (NCUA).*

It is wise to set up payments on loans as automatic payments, so you are never late. Interest can add up quickly. Loan payments can be set up with the bank in bill pay so they are made on the due date you set up. Your lender may also have an option where they will automatically pull the payment from your account. Just make sure that you have enough in your bank account when the funds are expected to come out to pay your loan.

Credit cards are a common type of unsecured loan. To obtain a credit card, you will need to complete an application. Lenders will require you to be at least eighteen years of age and provide proof of income to show that you can make the payments. Because of the high interest rates and late fees, credit cards, if not managed properly, can cause financial hardship and sometimes financial ruin. If you have trouble spending too much and are not able to pay the entire balance due by the due date every month, I strongly advise against using credit cards.

There are many types of credit cards available. If you choose to get a credit card, I recommend looking for a card that offers rewards. Different cards offer different benefits such as points you can redeem for a purchase (like airfare), cash back rewards, and discounts at retailers and restaurants. Rewards are tracked on the credit card website in the rewards section. These can be cashed in to buy something, pay your credit card bill, or receive the funds in cash. Look for a credit card that does not charge you an annual fee to own it and gives you rewards based on something you regularly buy, like groceries. These can help you save money. I do *not* recommend that you get more than one or two credit cards. These can be hard to juggle and keep track of especially when you are first starting out.

Most credit card companies charge compound interest *daily* on your average daily balance. This means interest can add up very quickly on a credit card balance if it is not paid in full each month. If you only pay the minimum amount on your credit card each month, the next month you will not only get charged interest on your purchases, but also interest on the interest that accumulated the previous month. Many people get into trouble with credit card debt because they only pay the minimum payment required each month. Credit card companies like customers who only pay the minimum because that is how they make more money. Now let's look at Figure 18.4 to see how to read a credit card statement. Credit card statements may be sent to you in the mail or you may view them online.

CREDIT CARD COMPANY STATEMENT

Account Summary/Payment Information | January 24 - February 23, 2025

Previous Balance	1,067.62
Payments and Other Credits	-1,716.86
Purchases and Adjustments	1,691.84
Fees Charged	0.00
Interest Charged	0.00
New Balance Total	1,042.60
Total Credit Line	7,500.00
Total Credit Line Available	6,457.40
Cash Credit Line	2,300.00
Portion of Credit Available for Cash	2,300.00
Statement Closing Date	2/23/2025
Days in Billing Cycle	31

New Balance Total	1,042.60
Current Payment Due	25.00
Total Minimum Payment Due	25.00
Payment Due Date	3/20/2025

LATE PAYMENT WARNING: If we do not receive your Total Minimum Payment by the date listed above, you may have to pay a late fee of $39.00 and your APRs may be increased up to the Penalty APR of 29.99%.

TOTAL MINIMUM PAYMENT WARNING: If you make only the Total Minimum Payment each period, you will pay more in interest and it will take you longer to pay off your balance. For Example:

If you make no additional charges using this card and each month you pay	You will pay off the balance shown on this statement in about	And you will end up paying an estimated total of
Only the Total Minimum Payment—$25.00	5 Years	1,471.00
$36.00	3 Years	$1,296.00

TOTAL BALANCE DUE— This is the total amount you owe as of the closing date (in this example Feb. 23, 2025. ALWAYS do your best to pay this entire balance no later than the Payment Due Date.
MINIMUM PAYMENT DUE—This is the minimum amount you need to pay to avoid an additional penalty.
LATE PAYMENT WARNING— If you pay after the due date (in this example 3/20/2025) you will have to pay a lot more.
BEWARE— If you only pay the Current Payment Due (which is the Minimum Payment Due) it will take you five years and cost $428.40 more (1,471.00-1,042.60). This is just for the New Balance of 1,042.60. If you make additional charges it will take longer and cost even more.

Figure 18.4 Sample Credit Card Statement

Note the blue boxes under the Late Payment Warning. If you only made the minimum payment of $25.00 each month, it would take you five years to pay off this balance and you would have to pay an additional $428.40 (1,471.00-1,042.60.) That could be a car payment. And that is provided you do not charge any more on this card.

The pages that come after the summary in your credit card statement outline your individual purchases and payments. *Always review the details!* Fraud, a type of identity theft, is commonplace. Some examples of fraud include gaining access to your account, opening an account in your name, cloning your card, and making purchases using your card number.

Another type of erroneous charge is when you are charged for the wrong amount or twice instead of once. If you see an inaccurate charge on a purchase you made, try to contact the company that charged your card and see if they will return your money. Credit card companies do have a form you can complete to "dispute the charge" but they will ask if you contacted the merchant who charged your card and what the result was. If you see charges on your account that you did not make, immediately contact your lender's fraud division and report it. Normally, they will cancel your card and issue you a new one. If you lose your card, ask your lender to freeze your card so no one can make purchases until you either find it or your lender can send you a new card. Many banks allow you to freeze your own card. Be diligent about reviewing your account. You won't be able to get your money back if you don't notice something is wrong.

You don't have to wait until the payment is due to make a payment. Making payments during the month will reduce your average daily balance and the amount you owe at the end of the month. For example, you could pay the balance on your credit card at the end of each week. This allows you to check for fraud, keep your spending under control, lower the amount due when the statement comes, and make sure you never miss a payment. If you always pay the balance before the statement date, this can increase your credit score. Your payment history—how often you pay your bills on time—is 35% of your total credit score, and the amounts you owe are 30% of your score. I strongly recommend that you set up an automatic payment to pay the balance in full each month, so you don't ruin your credit score or derail your finances. This can be set up on your bank's website for your credit card under automatic payments. Just make sure you have the funds in your bank account to cover the payment. If you pay before the statement date—the cutoff date, not the due date—it will show you do not owe anything on that card. Make sure you do not get yourself into credit card debt, because the compounding of interest daily makes this balance grow rapidly. Some people find credit card debt difficult to overcome. It is easy to whip out the card and buy something you want. However, it is better to save for items you want or need to purchase so you can pay off your card in full each month. Having too much debt can hurt your credit score, which we will examine in the next section, *Credit Scores*.

SUM IT UP

Understand and Manage Your Debt

- ➢ Know how your interest is calculated
- ➢ Know how frequently your interest is compounded
- ➢ Know the amount you will pay in total on the loan
- ➢ Know whether there is a prepayment penalty
- ➢ Check your credit card and loan statements every month
- ➢ Always pay in full before or by the due date each month
- ➢ Save money by paying extra on your loan if your loan allows prepayments

BRAINSTORM:

What loans do I currently have? List each loan, the interest rate, the due date, and whether or not prepayments can be made without a penalty.

....

....

....

....

What percentage of my earned income is going to pay debt (add up all of your debt payments for a month and divide it by your gross pay for the month). Note: this should not be more than 36%. To improve your financial position, strive to get this percentage even lower.

....

....

....

Am I able to pay extra to reduce interest and pay them off faster? How will I do this?

....

....

....

What steps have I taken to get my debt under control?

....

....

....

Do I pay off my credit card balance in full each month? If not, what steps can I take to eliminate carrying credit card debt?

....

....

....

19

Credit Scores

Your credit score is a measure of your ability to manage debt. Some people think it is a measure of your financial health, but a credit score does not look at earnings, savings, or net worth. A credit score only evaluates your debt. A Fair Isaac Corporation (FICO) score is a type of credit score that is commonly used to predict whether you could be expected to pay your loan payments on time. Your FICO score is calculated based on information on your credit reports. There are six credit reporting agencies, although most people just refer to the main three: Experian, Equifax, and TransUnion. Banks typically look at these three reports. Financial institutions and companies where you have credit cards, loans, or other credit accounts report to the credit bureaus about how long you have had credit, your credit limit—how much you can borrow—and your payment history—how often you pay on time. These reporting agencies also report if you have been looking to borrow more, such as shopping for a car loan.

As you can see in Figure 19.1, there are five categories that affect your FICO score. The two largest categories are Payment History (35%) and Amounts Owed (30%), followed by Length of Credit History (15%), Credit Mix (10%), and New Credit (10%). These combine to create your FICO score.

CREDIT SCORES

FACTORS THAT AFFECT YOUR CREDIT SCORE

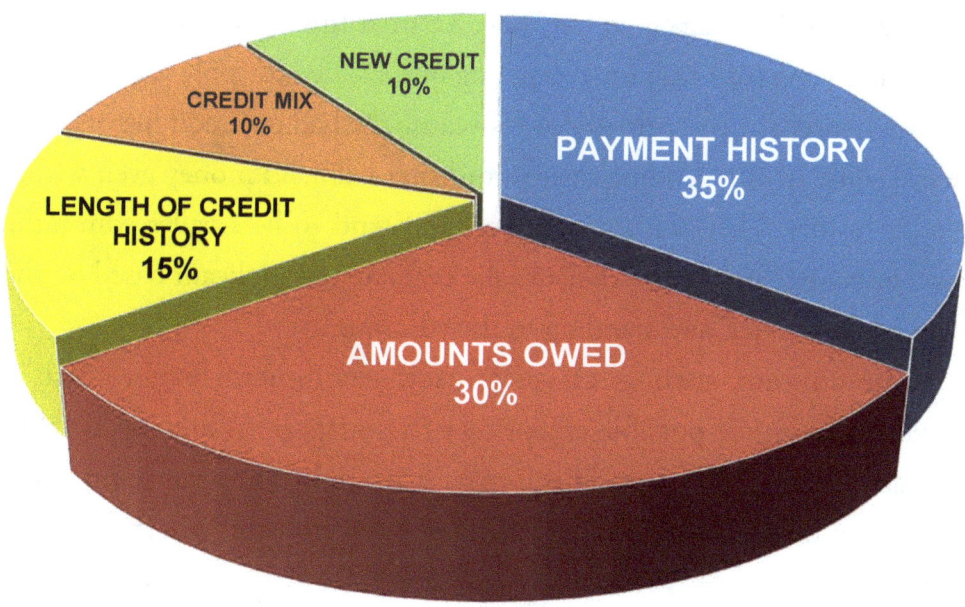

Figure 19.1 Factors that Affect Your Credit Score

Exceptional	800-850
Very Good	740-799
Good	670-739
Fair	580-669
Very Poor	300-579

Figure 19.2 FICO Score Ranking

Why should you care about your FICO score? FICO scores are not only used to determine if a lending institution will approve your loan request, but they can also determine how high your interest rate will be. If a bank decides to lend you money, but based on your FICO score there is a higher risk you will not pay back the loan, they will charge a higher interest rate to compensate for the fact that you are considered risky. Therefore, the people with the higher FICO scores get the lowest interest rates, and the people with the lowest FICO scores get the highest interest rate. It is all about risk. It is worth mentioning that people who avoid using credit may have a harder time getting a loan. I had an aunt who always paid cash for everything but decided to apply for a mortgage to buy a house. She was turned down because she had no credit history. There are still some smaller lending institutions that will lend money even without a credit history. They are not common and tend to be smaller community banks or savings and loans. They usually evaluate the applicant based on their financials, character, and standing in the community.

Some authors, such as Dave Ramsey, recommend paying cash for everything, with the possible exception of a mortgage. While I think this is good advice and recommend his books, it is important to note that credit scores may be used for more than merely determining whether you can borrow money.

Some insurance companies may charge a higher premium to those with lower FICO scores. The reasoning is that if someone is careful about the way they handle their debt, they are probably careful in other areas too. Therefore, they could be expected to present less risk for the insurance company. Sometimes potential employers, especially for jobs in accounting and finance, will run a credit check. They want to make sure the potential hire is careful with their own finances and does not have substantial debt.

There are ways you can build credit and help your score go up. When you are young, you have new credit (which accounts for 10% of your score) and a short time of credit history (which accounts for 15% of your score). Therefore, it is important to start building your credit at an early age. With each of my kids, we started with a $500 limit credit card (in their name) in high school. We agreed the card was only to be used for gas, and they would make sure they paid the full balance each month before the due date. Remember that amounts owed account for 30% of your score. Therefore, how much you use the credit card can affect your score. It is recommended that you keep credit card debt no more than 30% of your credit card limit.

If your credit card limit is $500, then you do not want to charge more than $150. Experts recommend that your total debt be no higher than 36% of your gross income, which includes debt for housing and cars. Interest and late payment penalties rack up quickly, and many people find themselves drowning in credit card debt. If you attend college, you should be aware that credit card companies target college students with credit card offers. Be smart. Choose cards carefully, do not have more than one or two cards, always pay in full by the due date, and remember that just because someone offers you something, it doesn't mean it is a good idea to accept it. Credit cards are **not** free money; use them sparingly and wisely. Refer to *What is Debt?* for more information on credit cards.

Credit bureaus sometimes make mistakes, so check your credit reports with all three agencies once a year and review for errors. You can do this for free at https://www.annualcreditreport.com. If you find an error, write to the credit agency explaining it is an error and what it should be. They should correct it if you can prove what you say is true. It is also possible to freeze your credit. Freezing your credit means that no credit can be given unless you unfreeze your accounts first. This protects against someone using your identity to get a loan or open accounts. To do this, contact each of the three agencies individually. This can be done online. You will set up a password that will be required for any new credit to be allowed. Later, you will need to unfreeze it if you want to borrow money—so make sure you know where you keep those passwords!

BRAINSTORM:

My current credit score is _____ which is Exceptional, Very Good, Good, Fair, or Very Poor

Have I reviewed my credit report for any errors and contacted the credit agencies about any errors found?

....

....

....

What steps can I take to improve my credit score?

....

....

....

Have I set up a password on my accounts so no one can take out a loan in my name?

....

....

....

#6 DEBT

ACROSS:

3. Loans that calculate interest this way usually cost more
6. A type of loan where the lender can take possession of the property if the loan is not paid
7. The property promised as security for a loan
11. A table detailing the periodic payments by how much was for principal and how much was for interest (2 words)
15. 35% of your credit score is based on this (2 words)
17. This type of interest is calculated on the principal and interest
18. Most credit cards compound interest with this frequency

DOWN:

1. A credit score is a measure of your ability to do this (2 words)
2. Something owed to someone else
4. Credit card companies often target this group (2 words)
5. 30% of your credit score is based on this (2 words)
8. A credit card is this type of debt
9. This type of interest is calculated only on the principal
10. The lender
12. Loans that allow these are better than loans that don't
13. The borrower
14. The amount borrowed
16. The name of a loan used to purchase real estate

20

Big Ticket Items: Buying and Leasing

According to the Bureau of Labor Statistics in 2023, Americans spent 32.9% of their total expenditures (money spent) on housing and 17% on transportation. These two categories alone account for nearly half of all money spent in the average household. Therefore, it is important to consider the cost when buying or leasing big ticket items like a house or car. Both homes and cars can either be leased or purchased, so let's look at some other relevant factors to weigh before making your decision.

One of the biggest expenses in the need category is housing. Many experts recommend that your monthly housing payment doesn't exceed 28% of your gross monthly income (the amount of pay before withholdings and taxes) and your total debt payments (payments on money you have borrowed), including housing and car payments, shouldn't exceed 36%. For example, if you make $4,500 per month, your housing payment should not exceed $1,260, and housing plus all other debt payments should not exceed $1,620. However, a more conservative approach would be to keep your monthly housing payment at or below 25% of your net income—your actual take home pay after deductions and taxes. Using this method, if your take home pay is $3,500 per month, your housing payment should be no more than $875. Some landlords and banks may allow you to spend more, but unless you want to struggle with money, I suggest you do not exceed the above recommendations. If you live in an area with a high cost of living or you do not make enough money to meet the suggested criteria, you may want to consider sharing your housing expenses with roommates. For a better understanding of loans refer to *What is Debt?*.

Leasing a Home

If you are going to rent an apartment, a condominium, or a house, you will need to sign a *lease*. Leases vary from place to place, so be sure to read the documents very carefully. If you plan to have a roommate (or more than one) to share the cost of the rental, it is advisable to have a separate, written agreement between you outlining how much each person pays, rules for how things will be handled, and what happens if one person doesn't pay their portion or wants to leave before the lease is up. Even good friends often have different ideas about how things will work. Putting it in writing will make sure everyone is on the same page. Some landlords will require a background check for each person on the lease.

You should always walk through the rental with the landlord prior to moving in. Note in writing and take photos to document any damage that exists.

Before signing a lease for a rental property, make sure the lease offers answers in writing to the following questions. Do not just take someone's verbal answer. It is not legally binding if it is not part of the written lease.

1. How much is the monthly rent and when is it due? Is there a late fee? Is there a grace period before the late fee kicks in?
2. How (cash, check, electronic), to whom, and where should rent payments be made (the address if mailed, hand delivered to an office, paid online)?

3. How much is required to be paid up front (such as security deposit, first month's rent, last month's rent) before moving in is permitted? What is required to get your security deposit back? To get back a security deposit, there should be no damage, and the rental should be clean and empty of everything that is not owned by the landlord (appliances supplied by the landlord need to stay with the rental). Some leases may also require the tenant to clean the carpets. If the landlord must repair damages, haul away junk left behind, or do extensive cleaning, the cost will come out of your security deposit. Prior to moving in always do a walk through with the landlord to document (including photos) any existing damages so you do not get charged for them when you move out.
4. Are pets permitted and is there an additional security deposit or higher rent if you have a pet? Make sure if you have a pet that you also find out the rules about what type of pet(s) are permitted and how many you can have. Ask about any specific rules for pets.
5. Are there any additional fees such as condominium fee or homeowners' association fee (also known as HOA)?
6. What utilities, if any, are included in the monthly rent? The landlord may pay some utilities like water, sewer, and trash, and the tenant may be responsible for paying gas, electric, and internet, but this will vary from place to place. *You will need to contact the utility companies to turn on the utilities you are responsible for.*
7. Who is responsible for lawn maintenance and snow removal?
8. Are appliances provided? If so, who is responsible for appliance repair? (Generally, if the landlord provides and owns the appliances, they will pay for repairs. If tenants bring their own appliances, they are responsible for any repairs.)
9. Is there a laundry hook-up in the rental? For appliances see number 8 above.
10. Does the lease require that you maintain a renter's insurance policy?

11. Are tenants permitted to make any changes (paint, wallpaper, flooring) to the property? Generally, changes are not permitted without written permission from the landlord in advance of any changes, and the changes are typically paid for by the tenant.
12. Where are tenants expected to park? Where are guests of tenants expected to park?
13. What are the rules about overnight guests? Generally, a landlord won't care if you have guests overnight for a few days if they follow the rules. If guests are going to be staying long-term, a landlord may require them to be on the lease. There may also be limits as to the number of people allowed to stay in the rental.
14. What are the rules for living in this rental?
15. Make sure it is in writing about when the landlord is permitted to enter the rental and under what conditions this is permitted.

Always shop around. Rents and lease terms vary greatly from place to place. If you get an opportunity to speak to current or former tenants, you may be able to get a good idea of how well the property is managed. Sometimes you can find online reviews, too. Tenants have rights which vary from state to state. Look online for federal and state tenant rights and know them before you sign any lease. These sites should also tell you who to contact if your rights are violated.

Buying a Home

When applying for a mortgage—loan to buy a house—the lender will require proof of income and a valid ID, such as a driver's license. Much of the additional information required will be a listing of the values of what you own, such as savings and proof of income. It's a good idea to get a pre-approval letter from a bank, so sellers will know you have been approved for a loan. The bank will have you complete an application to determine the amount they are willing to loan to you. In addition to proof of income and your ID, banks will also ask for bank statements to see how you will pay for the down payment, other outstanding loan statements, and tax returns. They should discuss how much you may need for a downpayment, and your expected interest rate and monthly payment.

Note that mortgages normally give you a choice of a 15-year mortgage or a 30-year mortgage, which is the length of time it will take to pay off the loan if you make the required payments each month. Find out how much the monthly payment will be for each. If you have a steady job that pays the same amount each month and you can comfortably afford the monthly payment, you may want to choose the 15-year mortgage so you can pay off your house in half the time. However, if the 15-year monthly payment is a stretch, or if your pay varies from month-to-month, you may want to consider the 30-year mortgage. This will make it more likely that you will not miss a payment—which only adds more interest and damages your credit score. If you opt for the 30-year, I suggest you choose a loan that permits extra payments without a prepayment penalty. Doing this will allow you to pay extra when you can and still pay off your loan early. The earlier you can pay off your loan, the more money you save. People purchasing a home will get a Closing Disclosure and a Loan Estimate (formerly called a Good Faith Estimate) which gives borrowers an overview of the estimated costs they will incur. It includes the interest rate, the loan costs, monthly payments, and a breakdown of your closing costs. Lenders are required to provide this within three business days of applying for a mortgage. This is a standardized form so you can easily compare other loan offers. I recommend using a realtor to help you find a house, help you line up inspections, negotiate the price, explain the closing documents, and what to expect at closing (when the buyer and the seller sign the final paperwork and exchange funds). You should also consider how much money you need to put aside for repairs and maintenance on a home, as well as insurance to protect your assets. For more information on mortgages, refer to the section *How Do Loans Work?*

Leasing a Car

Probably the biggest factor in deciding whether you should lease a car is how long you plan to drive it. A lease is basically a long-term car rental. If you plan to keep a car for five years or more, you will probably save money by purchasing a car rather than leasing one. Consumer Reports compares leasing versus buying at https://www.consumerreports.org/cars/buying-a-car/leasing-vs-buying-a-new-car-a9135602164/.

Some of the reasons you may want to lease:

- The ability to afford a more expensive car.
- Lower downpayment, warranties, and sometimes free maintenance.
- The freedom to change vehicles every two to three years.
- Only financing for the lease term (not the full price of the vehicle.)
- No need to trade in or sell.

Some of the reasons you may not want to lease:

- Don't own the car.
- May be more expensive in the long run
- May limit the number of miles included
- Often increases insurance premiums
- May have early termination fees
- May not be able to take to another state
- Can't customize
- Payments do not go toward the purchase
- Car payments continue
- Can't trade in or sell

To lease a car, you will need a driver's license (some require it to be a local license), proof of residence (such as a utility bill or bank statement), proof of income (such as a paystub, income tax return and/or bank statement), and proof of insurance (collision, comprehensive, and GAP, which covers the difference between the actual cash value of your car and your lease or loan). Most car lease companies also require you to be at least eighteen years of age and have a credit score of at least 670.

Before deciding to lease, know what you can afford to pay for the monthly payment as well as fuel, maintenance, and any extra charges and fees that are required by the lease. You should also know an estimate of how many miles you drive yearly (estimate a little higher than you think it actually is). When selecting a car, you want to choose one that maintains its value. Be sure to compare the cost of leasing with the cost of purchase. Go to https://www.edmunds.com/tco.html for a calculator to help you determine the cost of owning a car. You should know what interest rate you are paying, also known as the money factor. To convert the money rate stated in the lease to an equivalent interest rate, multiply by 2400. For example, if the money rate is .0030 the equivalent interest rate is 7.2% (.0030 * 2400). Familiarize yourself with lease terms (see below) and shop around. If this is your first time leasing, shopping around will also help you understand the process better. Negotiate the terms of the lease. You can negotiate the amounts as well as the mileage. Be sure to read the entire lease, including any fine print and ask questions about anything you don't understand. This is a contract, so you will be legally bound by it. You should also read other customers' reviews.

To determine if the monthly lease payment is fair consider the *one percent rule*. The calculation for the one percent rule is monthly lease payment/Manufacturer Suggested retail Price (MSPR) before taxes and fees. A fair monthly payment would be close to one percent. For example, if the MSRP of the car is $45,000, a fair monthly lease payment would be $450 (450/45,000=1%).

Lease Terms

Acquisition fee—up-front costs to set up the lease.

Buy out price—the amount you will need to pay at the end of the lease to purchase the car.

Capitalized cost restrictions—adjustments to lower the costs, such as trade-in or downpayment.

Capitalized costs—sales price of car.

Disposition fee—costs to cover cleaning and administrative tasks to prepare the returned vehicle for resale.

Drive off fees—can include Department of Motor Vehicles (DMV) registration fees, leasing fees, and security deposit.

GAP insurance—insures the difference between the actual cash value of your car and your lease or loan.

Lease term—the length of the lease, usually 24, 36, or 48 months.

Mileage allowance—the number of miles covered by the lease.

Money factor—interest rate on a lease.

Residual value—car's value at the end of the lease according to the lease agreement.

Security deposit—the amount of money collected up front in case the car is damaged and needs to be repaired. The security deposit should be returned to you at the end of the lease if the car is returned in good condition.

Buying a Car

As mentioned under Leasing a Car, one of the determining factors for whether to buy or lease is how long you plan to keep the car. Consumer Reports compares leasing and buying at https://www.consumerreports.org/cars/buying-a-car/leasing-vs-buying-a-new-car-a9135602164/.

To buy a car, you will need your driver's license, proof of car insurance, and your method of payment. In most states, you need to be at least eighteen years old to buy a car or take out an auto loan.

Before you purchase a car, you should do the following:

- Determine the type of car you need for your purposes.
- Research the cost to own, including repairs and cost of insurance. Go to Edmunds at https://www.edmunds.com/tco.html.
- Research safety records. The Insurance Institute for Highway Safety is a good place to find safety records. You can find the information at https://www.iihs.org/ratings.
- Research cars on Carfax at https://www.carfax.com.
- Know your budget and how much you can afford. See *How Do Loans Work?* and keep your total debt within the recommended percentage.
- Get preapproved for a car loan if you need to borrow money.
- Test drive cars. If you have never purchased a car before, visit lots of dealers so you learn more about buying a car.
- Go to Edmunds at https://www.edmunds.com/tmv.html to find out the true market value. It helps to have the Vehicle Identification Number (VIN).
- Ask for out-the-door price, which should include any hidden fees, and get written quotes.
- Negotiate. Based on your research on the internet and discussions with multiple dealers, know the fair price range. Often, if you mention research from the internet, they will pay closer attention to what you want.
- Be patient. If they think you are in a hurry to buy, they may pressure you to decide. Be willing to walk away if you aren't getting the deal you want. Walking away often gets their attention and tells them you are serious about your negotiation.

#7 BIG TICKET ITEMS

ACROSS:

3. In a negotiation, a willingness to do this will protect you from being taken advantage of (2 words)

8. This is a binding contract you will need to sign in order to lease a car or an apartment

9. An amount paid up front when renting a car or apartment (2 words)

10. Research this before buying a car (3 words)

11. Many experts recommend that this monthly payment not exceed 28% of your gross income or 25% of your net income

DOWN:

1. Use this rule to determine if a car lease payment is fair, which divides the monthly payment by the Mfg. suggested retail price (2 words)

2. Always do this and document any damages in writing before moving into a rental (2 words)

4. A document that must be given to you within three business days of applying for a mortgage or refinance (2 words)

5. To get the equivalent interest rate on a car lease, multiply this by 2400 (2 words)

6. Remember, nothing is legally binding if it is not in this format

7. If you plan to keep a car for five years or more, you will probably save money if you do this

12. This type of insurance is to cover the difference between the cash value of the car and your lease or loan balance in

21

The GPS of Finances

No one ever plans to fail; they just fail to plan.

—BENJAMIN FRANKLIN, United States of America Founding Father

We've talked about income, debt, saving, and spending. Now let's talk about how to stay on track, or the GPS of finances. Most of us are probably familiar with GPS, a voice that tells us whenever we make a wrong turn, "Recalculating route." You probably were in a car when that happened, and the driver got angry and argued with the GPS (maybe that driver is you.) It can be the same with budgets or any other tool we use to help us stay on track. A budget, also known as a spending plan, might seem restrictive, telling you what you can't do with your money. And let's be honest, who wants someone telling us what we can't do? However, a budget is really a tool that can help you make sure your actions are keeping you on track to accomplish your financial goals. It tells you when you are off course so you can make a correction. Budgets can seem like a lot of work, but as we will see, there are different ways you can budget and many of them are simple.

My mother used to use the envelope system for cash expenditures, like groceries, the newspaper boy, and the guy who mowed the lawn. It is decades old and easy to use if you want to deal in cash. Basically, she had an envelope for each of the categories for which she'd need money. When she got their paycheck, she would get cash from the bank to fill each envelope with the money to pay for those items. When the money in the envelope was spent, she was finished. She had met her budget. It was a surprisingly good way to ensure she didn't overspend or worry about overdraft fees on a checking account.

Some people still use the envelope system today. They make an envelope for each category. When they cash their paycheck, they put 100% of the cash in the envelopes. When the envelope is empty, they are done spending in that category until they get paid again and refill the envelopes. Others use the envelope method a little differently by using broad categories, such as Needs, Wants, Savings, and Charity. When they cash their paycheck, they put a percentage into each envelope. An example would be to put 50% in Needs, 20% in Wants, 20% in Savings, and 10% in Charity.

When my daughter was a teenager and got her first job, we set up a spreadsheet. We made columns for the categories, such as food, entertainment, gas, clothing, savings, charity, etc. On the first row we entered the amount she thought would be a reasonable amount under each category. When she spent money, she would log it onto her spreadsheet and the amount spent would automatically—with a formula—be subtracted from her budgeted amount, telling her how much she had left to spend that month. Refer to Figure 21.1 Sample Budget Using a Spreadsheet later in this section. Now, she is an adult and uses the budgeting app, You Need a Budget (YNAB). Some other budgeting apps are Goodbudget (envelope budgeting), EveryDollar, Empower Personal Dashboard, PocketGuard, and Honeydue. Different apps have different pricing options, and some offer free versions. Just make sure you understand the pricing, and if the app links to your bank account, that it uses banking protocols to safeguard your account. Some banks also offer budgeting tools to their customers.

DID YOU KNOW?

We use a double entry accounting system. The roots of double entry bookkeeping trace back to a Jewish community in the early 1300s. This method of keeping track of transactions gained in popularity when Luca Pacioli, an Italian, wrote a book published in 1494 detailing how to use this system. Basically, for every transaction there is one or more accounts that are *debited* (positive amount) and one or more accounts that are *credited* (negative amount) and when added together they must equal zero to balance. Today this is the standard for financial accounting worldwide.

In Figure 21.1 Sample Budget Using a Spreadsheet, the light blue columns are the transactions. On each line the debits must equal the credits. The Proof column is set up to add all of the transactions on each line to make sure they balance—equal zero. For example, if I withdraw or spend $25 (a credit or a negative in cash) to buy gas, I should enter $25 (a debit or a positive number) in the gas column.

THE GPS OF FINANCES

OCTOBER		CASH		TAKE HOME PAY	Gas	Eat Out	Fun	Clothes	Gifts	Emergency	Savings	Charity	PROOF
MONTHLY BUDGET				(800.00)	80.00	100.00	170.00	100.00	30.00	40.00	200.00	80.00	0.00
10/1/2019	Beginning Balance	Activity	Balance										
			125.00										
10/01/19	Gas	(25.00)	100.00		25.00								0.00
10/02/19	Pay	220.00	320.00	(220.00)									0.00
10/05/19	Concert	(230.00)	90.00			50.00	180.00						0.00
10/08/19	Gas	(15.00)	75.00		15.00								0.00
10/09/19	Pay	220.00	295.00	(220.00)									0.00
10/15/19	Gas	(20.00)	275.00		20.00								0.00
10/16/19	Pay	250.00	525.00	(250.00)									0.00
10/17/19	Clothing Store	(110.00)	415.00					110.00					0.00
10/17/19	Food	(25.00)	390.00			25.00							0.00
10/22/19	Gas	(20.00)	370.00		20.00								0.00
10/22/19	Food	(30.00)	340.00			30.00							0.00
10/22/19	Coffee	(5.00)	335.00			5.00							0.00
10/23/19	Pay	220.00	555.00	(220.00)									0.00
10/24/19	Coffee	(5.00)	550.00			5.00							0.00
10/24/19	Breakfast	(10.00)	540.00			10.00							0.00
10/24/19	Emergency Fund	(40.00)	500.00							40.00			0.00
10/31/19	Savings	(200.00)	300.00								200.00		0.00
10/31/19	Charity	(80.00)	220.00									80.00	0.00
MONTH TOTALS		95.00		(910.00)	80.00	125.00	180.00	110.00	0.00	40.00	200.00	80.00	0.00
OVER / UNDER BUDGET				(110.00)	0.00	25.00	10.00	10.00	(30.00)	0.00	0.00	0.00	(95.00)

Figure 21.1 Sample Budget Using a Spreadsheet

The budget amounts for the month are in the green row at the top. The bottom green row is the difference between the actual amounts spent and the amounts budgeted. Credits in the bottom row are good because it means we either had more income or less expenses than what we budgeted. Positive numbers in the bottom row mean we either had less income or spent more than we had planned. The over or under budget total in the proof column tells us overall how we did this month. In this case, we earned $110 more than expected and we spent a net of $15 more than we had planned, which left us $95 ahead of what we had planned overall (110-15=95). We should always review what happened. We can see that we spent too much on eating out, fun, and clothes. If we had not made more pay than we expected, we would have been over budget. To get back on track, we would need to cut back in those areas next month. Remember, a budget is only a useful tool if you evaluate the results. If you plug in numbers and never review them, you are not making the necessary corrections to get back on track.

Note the savings category in the budget. This is critical if you want to grow your money. Many employers make it easy for you to save by allowing you to say you want a certain amount deducted from your pay each time and deposited into your savings account. If you are living on your own, you should also have an emergency fund to handle unexpected expenses. If you don't currently have money set aside to cover emergencies, I recommend you put some aside each month to build one. You never know when you may have a medical emergency, a car repair, or some other unexpected bill. If you have an emergency fund, you will have money set aside to use, so an unforeseen expense won't derail your finances. Most people who do not use a budget cannot say for sure how much they have spent on each category. In fact, a lot of people wouldn't be able to tell you how much they spent in total. When we only spend a few dollars here and there it doesn't seem like a big deal, but it all adds up, and it's easy to lose track of how much we are spending. If you keep making wrong turns and ignoring your GPS, you will eventually get lost. Budgets help us stay on top of our spending and savings, and like a GPS, they can help us get where we want to go.

DEEPER DIVE

In accounting, your debits need to equal your credits. The list below shows what the normal balance is in each part of the financial statements. There are a couple of exceptions, such as accumulated depreciation (in the asset section) has a normal credit balance (it decreases the value of the asset) and sales discounts (in the income section) has a normal debit balance (it decreases the value of a sale).

Assets (what you own)	Debit
Liabilities (what you owe)	Credit
Equity (net worth)	Credit
Income	Credit
Expenses	Debit

To increase the balance in an account with a normal debit balance you would enter a debit; to decrease the balance you would enter a credit. The opposite is true for accounts with a normal credit balance. For example, when we pay rent, we decrease our cash (credit) and increase our rent expense (debit). Whether a debit or a credit is good or bad depends on the account. You want to see debits in your cash account which means you are adding cash, but you want to see credits in your income account because it means your income is increasing. It is good to see your assets, equity, and sales increase. It is good to see your liabilities and your expenses decrease.

BRAINSTORM:

These are the categories I need to use in my budget. (Note a column for Other can be used to record expenditures that are not listed as a separate category—just be sure there is a budgeted amount for Other).

Category	Budget Amount

#8 BUDGET

ACROSS:

3. Always make sure you set aside money for this
5. This system of bookkeeping means the debits and credits must equal (2 words)
7. Budgets are only useful if you do this to the results
8. Also called a spending plan, this helps you stay on track to meet your financial goals

DOWN:

1. Other ways to set up a budget are to use a _____ or a budgeting app
2. In this method of budgeting, you allocate cash into different categories
4. In bookkeeping, this is a negative number
5. In bookkeeping, this is a positive number

22

You Snooze, You Lose!

Would you agree that the only person who can take care of the older person you will someday be—is the younger person you are now?

—AUTHOR UNKNOWN

Now that we have discussed how to measure our progress, let's talk about long-term planning for retirement. If you do a good job saving for retirement, this account will eventually become one of your biggest assets.

A retirement plan offered by your employer is an investment account designed for you to be able to invest in your future so you will have money for retirement. Because retirement usually starts between sixty-five and seventy years of age, it is easy to put off planning. As many older people are finding out, retirement preparation should begin when you are young. If you wait until you are older to start saving for retirement, you have missed the most important advantage of youth—time! The more time invested, the more your money can grow. Also, the best time to save is when you are young and do not have all the expenses that typically come in later adulthood when raising a family. And the best time to form good habits is now. If your retirement contributions automatically come out of your pay, you will soon get used to not having it to spend and won't think about it. Here are some things to consider.

1. **Money grows with time**. In the section *Formula to Make Money Grow*, we learned that the longer your money is invested, the more money it makes. See Figure 22.1 Growth of Account Over Time later in this chapter.

2. **Most retirees will be eligible to collect social security.** Social security is money paid each month to retirees who signed up to receive social security benefits. Remember the social security taxes that come out of your paycheck at 6.2%? Those taxes are collected for social security benefits. The amount you are entitled to is based on how long you worked, how much you made when you were working, and at what age you signed up to receive social security; the earliest is age sixty-two. In 2025, the average amount of social security paid out to retirees who have reached full retirement age is $1,981 per month. Most retirees are also on Medicare for their health insurance and the premium is deducted from their social security check. In 2025 that amount is on average $185. So this nets to $1,796, or about the same amount as someone working a full-time job at $10 per hour. Will this be enough to cover your needs and wants in retirement? See the Did You Know box in this section to learn more about social security.

3. **Pensions are rare these days**. A pension, also called a defined benefit plan, is money employers invest to pay their employees when they retire. Because very few employers offer pensions now, this money is not something most people can rely on in retirement.

4. **Prices usually go up.** Inflation is something everyone should consider when planning their retirement. By the time you retire, it will cost more to live so your dollar will buy less than it does today. Even though Social Security benefits are adjusted for cost of living, will it be enough?

5. **No one knows for certain what their health will be like when they retire**. If you have health issues during retirement, the cost of

care and medications could take most if not all your social security check. Will you have other money available to pay for health and other needs? In *Benefits*, we discussed HSA accounts. If you have an HSA account, you are not *required* to pull money out of this account for medical bills. If you can, avoid withdrawing from this account for as long as you can and think of it as part of your retirement plan. The money will grow tax free and be available to help with medical bills when you are older.

6. **Taxes are a fact of life**. If you have other taxable income—such as wages, self-employment income, interest/dividends, or withdrawal from a traditional 401k or IRA—that when combined with your social security benefits are between $25,000 and $34,000, you may have to pay tax on up to 50% of your social security benefits. If it is more than $34,000, up to 85% of your social security benefits may be taxable. (*Discussions happen from time to time in Congress about changing the law to no longer tax social security, but as of this writing, social security is taxed as outlined above*).

7. **Roth accounts must be at least five years old to avoid taxes**. If your Roth account was opened more recently and is not yet five years old, you will be taxed on all the earnings you withdraw. You are never taxed on your contributions. If you opened your Roth account more than five years ago, you will not be taxed on any of the money you withdraw, including the earnings.

8. **Most employers will put money into your retirement account**. Some employer retirement plans—such as a 401k plan, also known as a defined contribution plan—require you to contribute to your retirement account to get a match from your employer. Other plans require the employer to contribute a certain percentage even if you do not contribute. If you do not opt into a retirement account, you are losing all the "free" money from your employer. Do you really want to leave "free" money on the table? If your employer does

not offer a retirement account, you can always open an Individual Retirement Account (IRA) and deposit money toward retirement. There are limits to how much you can contribute, which typically changes each year.

9. **You snooze, you lose**. This saying applies to retirement accounts. No one ever gets to retirement and regrets investing money early, but many get to retirement and regret they didn't start earlier. Saving for retirement early can be the difference between doing what you want to do in retirement and doing what you must do to support yourself.

DEEPER DIVE

- The social security taxes withheld from your pay are not saved in an account specifically for you.
- A calculation based on past earnings and the age you start collecting determines the amount you are entitled to receive at retirement.
- The social security taxes collected are used to pay the older generation's retirement (each generation paying social security taxes is paying for the generation collecting social security).
- The social security system depends on each successive generation to have enough people paying social security taxes. If there are not enough people paying in, you may get a smaller piece of the pie at retirement.
- The federal government is permitted to use social security tax money for other expenditures, but they must pay it back with interest.
- People can file for social security benefits as early as age sixty-two, but they will not receive the full amount calculated

from their lifetime earnings history. They must reach full retirement age, which is sixty-seven for those born in 1960 and after. Social security pays more per month if you wait until the age of seventy to claim it.
- ➤ Social security recipients may get a cost-of-living adjustment (COLA) to keep pace with inflation. It is tied to the CPI-W, the price index for consumer goods and services, and is adjusted annually. If prices have remained steady, they may not get an increase.
- ➤ Members of U.S. Congress do pay into social security and have done so since 1984, along with the rest of the federal workforce.
- ➤ Undocumented immigrants cannot get social security. Non-citizens who live and work in the U.S. legally can qualify for social security, but they also must pay.
- ➤ Over their lifetime, most people get more from social security and medicare than they pay in FICA social security and FICA medicare taxes.

Information from AARP

You don't have to be financially secure to start saving; you have to start saving to be financially secure.
—VANESSA PATRICK, PhD quoted in *Psychology Today*.

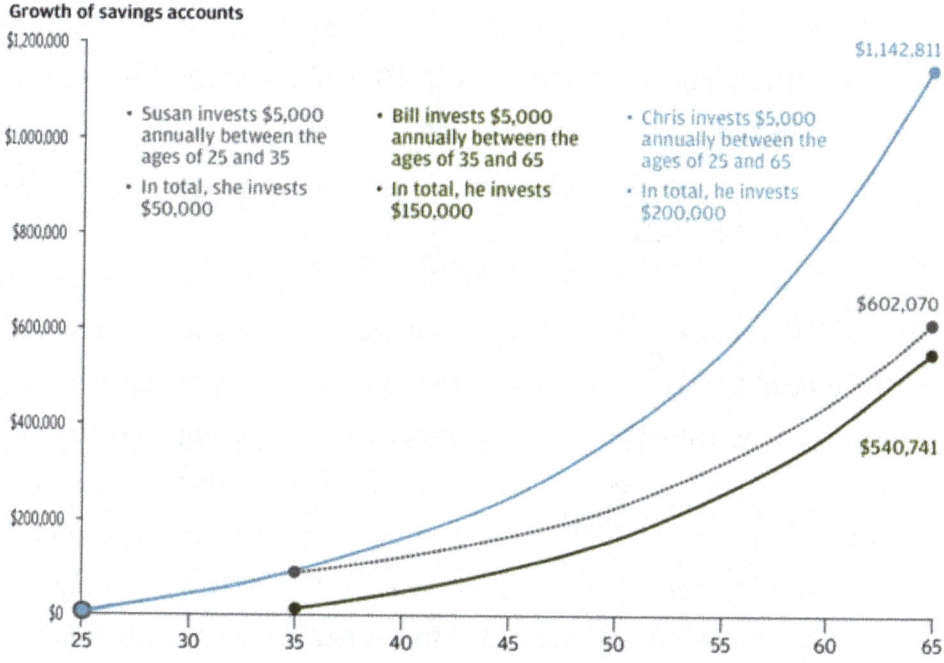

Figure 22.1 Growth of Account Over Time
Chart created by JP Morgan Asset Management as seen on Lifehack
https://www.lifehack.org

Let's look at Figure 22.1. Susan and Chris both invest $5,000 annually between the ages of twenty-five and thirty-five. You can see they both have the same amount of money at age thirty-five. Then Susan stops investing. Her investment of $50,000 grew to $602,070 by age sixty-five. Chris continued to invest $5,000 each year through age sixty-five, and his investment of $200,000 grew to $1,142,811. Chris invested only $150,000 more than Susan, but his investment at age sixty-five was worth $540,741 more than hers.

Now let's look at Bill's investment of $150,000. Bill *waited.* Bill invested $100,000 more than Susan did, and he invested for twenty more years than Susan, but at age sixty-five, Bill's investment was worth $61,329 *less* than Susan's investment—all because Bill waited to start. Bill invested $50,000 less than Chris, but Bill's investment was worth $602,070 *less* than Chris's investment, again because Bill waited to start.

To contribute or save money in a retirement account, you must have earned income. If you remember in the section *I Work Hard for the Money*, earned income is money you earn by working. Individual Retirement Accounts are called IRAs. There are two types of IRAs. One is a traditional—tax-deferred—IRA, which means you can deduct the amount you contribute from your taxable income and lower your current taxes. All the money contributed—plus all the growth—will be taxable when you start to pull the money out during retirement. The other type of IRA is the Roth IRA. You will not get any tax break for your contributions now, but when you pull money out, everything is tax free. Your contributions are tax free because you already paid tax on that money. And in a Roth IRA, all the growth is also tax-free money (as long as your account has existed for at least five years) even though you never paid taxes on this portion. Because retirement accounts have different tax rules, they must be identified as traditional IRA or Roth IRA, and the money in these accounts can't be co-mingled with each other or other accounts, such as a savings account.

In addition to IRAs, many employers offer a retirement plan to help their employees save for retirement, and many of those plans have a Roth option in addition to the tax deferred option. Figure 22.2 shows some of the more popular retirement accounts with a general description of each.

PLAN	SUMMARY OF PLAN
401k	Designed for "For Profit" businesses in the private sector Defined contribution plan Funded by employee contributions Often comes with some employer contributions too Contribution limits in 2025: $23,500
403b	Like the 401k plan except for government and "non-profit"
457	Like a 401k plan except for state and local government employees Contribution limit in 2025: $23,500
Simple IRA	Retirement plan for small employers Employer must match dollar for dollar what an employee contributes, up to 3% of the employee's pay or pay a flat 2% of the employee's pay regardless of how much the employee contributes Contribution limits in 2025: $16,500 with an additional catch up amount of $3,500 for those ages 50 – 59 or 64 and older; ages 60-63 are allowed an additional $5,250 for catch up amount
SEP IRA	Like a Simple IRA but much higher contribution limits Only employers can contribute and the percentage can vary from 0% to 25% Contribution limits for 2025: cannot exceed the lesser of 25% of employee's pay or $70,000
	Note: plans differ among employers. Check with human resources for specific details about your plan. All of the above plans are eligible for the Roth option— consult your plan to see if Roth is included.

Figure 22.2 Types of Retirement Plans

Some retirement plans also offer free financial advice from a licensed financial advisor. Check with your human resources department to see if your plan offers this. Deciding how much money to put into which funds can be confusing, so take advantage of help from a financial planner if this option is available to you. Figure 22.3 explains the differences between traditional and Roth retirement accounts.

Retirement is wonderful if you have two essentials—
much to live on and much to live for.
—AUTHOR UNKNOWN

FAQs	TAX DEFERRED (TRADITIONAL)	ROTH
Are contributions tax deductible?	Yes Note some limits may apply to how much you can deduct—visit www.irs.gov	No
Can I contribute to both Traditional and Roth?	Yes, you can contribute to Traditional and Roth if Roth is available in your employer's plan.	Yes, you can contribute to Traditional and Roth if Roth is available in your employer's plan.
How much can I contribute?	The maximum contributions allowed over all IRAs in 2025: Not to exceed earned income Under age 50 can contribute $7,000 Over age 50 can contribute $8,000 For other plan limits—see the earlier table on retirement plans.	The maximum contributions allowed over all IRAs in 2025: Not to exceed earned income Under age 50 can contribute $7,000 Over age 50 can contribute $8,000 For other plan limits—see the earlier table on retirement plans.
Can I contribute to an IRA if I also have a plan at work?	Yes, but the tax-deductible portion of the contribution may be limited. Visit www.irs.gov	Yes, but only within the income limitations. Visit www.irs.gov
Are the amounts my employer contributes to my plan taxable?	Yes, employer contributions will be taxable when you withdraw them. They are considered tax-deferred	Yes, employer contributions will be taxable when you withdraw them. They are considered tax-deferred
Are there taxes and penalties for early withdrawal?	Before age 59½ - • Pay taxes on both contributions and earnings withdrawn • Pay a 10% penalty • There are some exceptions—visit www.irs.gov After age 59½ - • Pay taxes on both contributions and earnings withdrawn • No penalty	Before age 59½ - • Contributions can be withdrawn at any time tax free and penalty free at any age. • Earnings withdrawn before the account is 5 years old are taxable and subject to a penalty • There are some exceptions—visit www.irs.gov After age 59½ - • Earnings withdrawn will have no penalty • Earnings will only be subject to income taxes if the account is less than 5 years old.
Am I able to borrow from my retirement account?	You may <u>not</u> borrow from an IRA You may be able to borrow from an employer retirement account, but it depends upon the terms of your company's plan—see human resources for information	You may <u>not</u> borrow from an IRA You may be able to borrow from an employer retirement account, but it depends upon the terms of your company's plan—see human resources for information
Am I able to move money from one type of retirement account to the other	Yes, if in a traditional IRA, but you will have to pay taxes on the money. After you pay taxes and move to Roth, all of the money in the account, including earnings, will be tax free	Do not move Roth money to a tax deferred account – taxes were already paid
Am I required to pull a certain % of money out by a certain age? This is called RMD (Required Minimum Distribution)	Yes, this is because the IRS wants to collect the taxes on amounts that have not yet been taxed If you turn 73 between 2023-2032 you must begin taking RMDs when you turn 73; from 2033 and beyond you start when you turn 75	There are no RMDs for owners of a Roth. Inherited Roth accounts generally require the beneficiaries to withdraw all of the money within 10 years.
For more information on retirement plans, visit www.dol.gov What You Should Know About Your Retirement Plan		

Figure 22.3 Differences Between Traditional and Roth Retirement Accounts

Some Additional Facts About Employers' Retirement Accounts

Vesting Schedule

A vesting schedule is a prorated way for an employee to earn access to certain employer benefits, such as retirement plan match, stock options, or a pension. Employers use this as an incentive for employees to stay longer in their employment. The vesting schedule is detailed in the company's plan, and the human resources department should be able to answer any questions about it. If you are vested, it means the money belongs to you. You are always 100% vested in contributions you make with your own money. However, what the employer contributes may not be considered "fully vested" until you work a certain amount of time.

For example, let's say you work for a company that matches your contribution dollar for dollar up to 4% if you invest 5%. If your income is $50,000 and you invest $2,500, your employer will contribute a $2,000 match into your retirement account. If you are fully vested right away, the $4,500 in your account belongs to you. But let's say that the vesting schedule is different, and you are vested 25% after one year, an additional 25% after two years, and fully vested after three years. (Note: the vesting schedule starts when you are eligible to participate in the plan, not when you are first hired. Your employer's plan will state how long you are required to work before you are eligible, and vesting schedules vary from employer to employer.) If each year you contribute $2,500 and your employer matches $2,000, Figure 22.4 shows what you get to keep if you leave the company after one, two, or three years, using the vesting percentages noted above, and how much money you would leave behind.

If Employee leaves employment Vested for:	Employee Share of Account	Employer Share of Account	Vested portion of Employer Share of Account	Total amount owned by employee	Amount of money left behind
Year One	2,500	2,000	2,000* 25%= 500	$3,000	**$1,500**
Year Two	5,000	4,000	4,000* 50%=2,000	$7,000	**$2,000**
Year Three	7,500	6,000	6,000*100%=6,000	$13,500	**$0**

Figure 22.4 Example of How a Vesting Schedule Works

If you leave your employer before you are fully vested, the amount of the employer's share you leave behind is called a *forfeiture*. You forfeit or give up that amount of money because you did not stay long enough to become fully vested. Forfeited money is then moved to a forfeiture account, which the employer can use to pay future fees or matches.

Retirement Account Rollover

A rollover is when you move money from one eligible retirement account to another. For example, if you switch jobs, you may choose to rollover your former 401k to your new employer's 401k, or if you leave the workforce, you may want to rollover your 401k to an IRA. (Note: there are pros and cons as well as possible tax and penalty implications, so do your research and consider the specifics of your situation before deciding.) There are two types of rollovers: direct and indirect. A *direct rollover* is where the money moves directly from one retirement account to another without the owner of the account ever having possession of the money. An *indirect rollover* is when the money is moved out of the old account and sent to the owner, who then deposits it into the new account. A direct rollover protects the individual from taxes and penalties. With an indirect rollover, one hundred percent of the money from the old account must be deposited into the new account within sixty days to avoid taxes and penalties. The process begins by first opening the new account. If you move money to a new employer's plan, make sure you are eligible to participate in their plan before starting the process. Some employers require a waiting period before an employee is eligible to join their plan. Often, the new plan can facilitate the rollover from the old plan and the HR department can assist you with the necessary paperwork and guide you through the process.

Retirement Account Loan

Some retirement plans permit you to borrow from your retirement account. You need to ask HR if your plan allows loans. Loans only apply to company-sponsored plans because loans are not permitted on Individual Retirement Accounts. While this might sound great if you need money, you should beware of the tax consequences, especially if you do not pay the loan back. If you are married, your spouse will also need to sign that they are okay with you taking a loan from your retirement account.

When you borrow money from your retirement account, you should be given an amortization schedule detailing the amount to be repaid, the interest rate, and the total monthly payment. The payment will go into your retirement account after tax dollars—meaning you pay taxes on that money. Someday, when you start taking distributions from your account, those dollars will be taxed like the rest of the money in the account. If the amounts are small, the tax impact will be insignificant. The repayments are normally withheld from your paycheck. Be sure to ask what happens if you leave their employment and still have an outstanding loan. Depending on the plan, the balance due may be withdrawn from your retirement account. This lowers the account balance you have saved for retirement, and that full amount is now taxable in the year the money was taken out to repay the loan. If you are under fifty-nine and six months, you will not only have to pay taxes on the full amount of the unpaid balance, but you will also be assessed a 10% penalty. If you are over fifty-nine and six months, you will not have to pay a penalty, but you will still be assessed taxes.

Retirement Account Transfer

A *retirement account transfer* is when you move money from one retirement account to another retirement account of the same type but to a different financial institution, or custodian. To do this, ask your current financial institution for a trustee-to-trustee transfer.

Retirement Account Distribution

A *distribution* from a retirement account is a withdrawal of money. A distribution can be taken from any type of retirement account. There are some exceptions (see https://www.irs.gov) but generally, if you withdraw money from your account before age fifty-nine and six months, you will have to pay a 10% penalty. If you make a distribution after age fifty-nine and six months, you will not be subject to a penalty. A *qualified distribution* means the distribution will incur no penalty. A *non-qualified distribution* is a distribution that will incur a 10% penalty. Refer to Figure 22.3 Differences Between Traditional and Roth Retirement Accounts earlier in this chapter for information on whether your distribution will be taxable.

Required Minimum Distribution or RMD

The law doesn't permit you to leave your retirement money in your account indefinitely because the government wants the income taxes due on the money. Currently the law requires that you begin taking distributions out of your account the year following your seventy-second birthday (or age seventy-three if you reach age seventy-two after Dec. 31, 2022). These requirements are called *required minimum distributions* or RMDs. It is particularly important to calculate the correct amount you need to withdraw and do so by the due date. If you withdraw too little or wait until after the due date, you may have to pay a 25% excise tax on the amount not distributed as required. The RMD rules apply to Individual Retirement Accounts (traditional/pretax),

SEP IRAs, SIMPLE IRAs, 401k plans, 403b plans, 457b plans, profit sharing plans, other defined contribution plans, and Roth beneficiaries. Money held in Roth accounts are exempt from Required Minimum Distributions if the original owner is still alive. Beneficiaries of Roth accounts could have RMDs depending on a number of factors which are beyond the scope of this book. Rules also change from time to time, so always discuss with a financial advisor. Beneficiaries who are required to take RMDs can also be assessed additional taxes if they do not withdraw the correct amount by the due date.

Beneficiaries

As Benjamin Franklin observed, "In this world, nothing is certain except death and taxes." In *Benefits*, I briefly mentioned the term beneficiary regarding an HSA account. A beneficiary is the person or persons who will get the money in your account when you die. A primary beneficiary is the first person or entity who gets the funds. If the primary beneficiary has died or is unwilling or unable to accept, the money would go to a secondary beneficiary. You can name more than one person as primary (and secondary), and the percentage each would get. It is best to name beneficiaries for all your accounts, but it is especially important for a retirement account, since it typically grows for a long period of time and can be a sizable asset.

BRAINSTORM:

Do I have a retirement account set up?

....

....

....

Does my employer contribute to my account?

....

....

....

Do I have a Roth account?

....

....

....

How much do I contribute to my retirement and how often?

....

....

....

How would I be able to contribute more?

....

....

....

Do I have an HSA?

....

....

....

If so, do I contribute the maximum permitted each year?

....

....

....

Does my employer contribute to my HSA? If so, how much?

....

....

....

#9 RETIREMENT

ACROSS:

1. When your employer adds money to your retirement plan, it is called a _____
3. Currently RMDs are _____ for owners of a Roth (2 words)
6. With a traditional retirement account, you are not taxed when you make these
9. The biggest advantage you have is to invest in your retirement when you are young because money grows with _____
11. A prorated way for employees to access certain employer benefits like a retirement plan match, stock options, or a pension (2 words)
13. When you withdraw money from a traditional retirement account, on what portion will you have to pay tax?
15. When money buys less because prices went up

DOWN:

2. These are an important thing to consider in retirement planning
4. A 401k, a 403b, and a 457 are examples of this (2 words)
5. With this type of retirement account, you are taxed when you make contributions
7. When the IRS requires you to pull out a certain amount of money each year from your retirement account after you reach a certain age—called a Required Minimum _____
8. Money employers invest to pay their employees when they retire (not as common today)
10. An IRA stands for an _____ Retirement Account
12. What kind of health insurance allows you to save and earn tax free?
14. If your Roth account is at least five years old, how much of your withdrawal is taxable?
15. You may not borrow money from this type of account

23

Net Worth: What's the Big Deal?

You have to measure what you want more of.

—CHARLES COONRADT, President and CEO of The Game of Work

Earlier we said a person's true value doesn't have anything to do with money. So, as we talk about net worth, I want you to remember this tells you where you stand financially, not your value as a person. Your net worth is a better indicator of how you are doing than the money you make from your job. Think of it this way, your net worth is the *BIG* picture and what you make from your job is just one piece. So, let's start with how net worth is calculated, and then we will look at some examples.

Net worth (also known as book value or shareholders'/owners' equity in business) is part of the balance sheet. The basic financial statements are the *balance sheet* (also known as the statement of financial position) and the *income statement* (also known as the profit & loss statement). Think of the balance sheet as a snapshot on a given date, whereas the income statement is more like a video showing us what was going on during the year. The balance sheet totals are from the beginning of time. The income statement is only for a year.

Balance Sheet

The categories found on the balance sheet are assets, liabilities, and equity (also known as your net worth). To find your Net Worth, follow this *formula*:

Assets (what you own) − *Liabilities* (what you owe) = *Net Worth* (Equity)

On the balance sheet, list all your assets and their values (what they are worth now). Then list all your liabilities, such as credit cards and loans (principal only on loans). Your total assets minus your total liabilities equals your net worth.

DEEPER DIVE

There are different types of assets. Current assets are usually listed at their actual value. An example of a current asset is cash. Fixed assets are listed at lower of cost or market value. An example of a fixed asset is a car. When listing your fixed assets find out what they are worth now. You may have paid $20,000 for your car, but if you have owned it for four years, its market value is now lower. It is no longer worth the amount you paid for it. Now it may only be worth $4,000. On your balance sheet you would enter your car at $4,000, not $20,000. Assets like cars not only depreciate (lose value) over time, but also require money to keep them maintained. A car is not an investment because it does not make money for you. An exception would be an antique car that would appreciate (increase in value).

Another way to think about net worth is this: If you had to sell everything you own and pay off all your loans and credit cards, what would you have left? This is the amount that truly belongs to you—not a bank or other lender.

PERSON A		PERSON B	
House	2,000,000	House	480,000
Car-2024 Porsche	160,000	Car – 2022 Honda CR-V	26,800
Cash & Investments	100,000	Cash & Investments	150,000
TOTAL ASSETS	**2,260,000**	**TOTAL ASSETS**	**656,800**
Mortgage on House	1,800,000	Mortgage on House	360,000
Car Loan	145,000	Car Loan	10,000
Other loans/credit cards	250,000	Other loans/credit cards	0
TOTAL LIABILITIES	**2,195,000**	**TOTAL LIABILITIES**	**370,000**
NET WORTH	**65,000**	**NET WORTH**	**286,800**

Figure 23.1 Comparison of Two Net Worth Calculations

In this country, we often attach value to a person based on how rich we think they are. This is not only a terrible way to treat people, but as you can see in Figure 23.1, we can't tell how wealthy a person is by looking at things like the house they live in or the car they drive. Look at the house and the car Person A owns compared to what Person B owns. Just by looking, which person would you think is wealthier? Now look at each person's net worth. Who do you think does a better job of managing their money? Who do you think would be better prepared to handle an emergency, the loss of a job, or a medical issue? Person B is $221,800 wealthier than Person A.

You may not have many assets yet. However, it is important for you to understand how to calculate your net worth so when you do have assets, you will know where you stand. Even if you rent, you can still build net worth. Keep reading to see ways to increase your net worth.

DEEPER DIVE

Businesses often use a third financial statement called the *statement of cash flows* which details where the cash came from and where the cash went. This is different than a cash projection. A *cash projection* is a forecast of where the money will come from and where it will go in the future.

Income Statement

Now, let's look at what we find in an income statement. The income statement's categories are income and expenses—these categories can be broken down into smaller groups, but for simplicity's sake, we are just going to talk about two main groups for individuals. Income is money coming in. Usually, this is the pay you receive from a job, but it could also be passive income as discussed in *Money That Works Hard for Me*. Expenses are things that you pay for such as rent, utilities, food, interest on loans, etc. We call the difference between your income and your expenses your *net income or loss*. What you do with your money can affect your net income (loss). If your expenses are less than your income, you will make a profit. If they are more, you will have a loss.

Tracking your income and expenses is extremely helpful for meeting your goals. If you make a budget, as discussed in *The GPS of Finances*, and compare your actual income and expenses to your budget, you can quickly see if you get off track and need to make a correction. You are less likely to achieve your goals if you are not measuring your progress.

A *big* mistake a lot of people make is spending more when they make more. In other words, every time they get a raise, they think they need a bigger house or a fancier car. Often, they do it to impress people, rather than because of a true need. Smart people don't worry about impressing others. They save and invest their raises to improve their financial position and increase their net worth. If you save and invest enough, your passive income will grow and may eventually be able to pay for your living expenses, so you do not have to work. The more expenses you have, the harder it is to accumulate enough passive income to pay for them.

The ways to increase your net worth are:

- ✓ Increase your income
- ✓ Decrease your expenses
- ✓ Save and invest more in assets that generate more income
- ✓ Buy assets that appreciate
- ✓ Pay off or pay down your debt

BRAINSTORM:

Calculate your Net Worth

House	
Car	
Cash & Investments	
Other assets	
TOTAL ASSETS	

Mortgage on House	
Car Loan	
Other Loans and Credit Cards	
TOTAL LIABILITIES	
NET WORTH	

What actions can I take now to increase my Net Worth and what will be the value of the change?

Changes to make	Value of the change

DEEPER DIVE

At the end of the year, the income statement is closed, and the profit or loss is added to the equity section of the balance sheet. The balance sheet accounts on January 1 will be the same as they were on December 31, with the exception of equity. For example, if you had $1,000 in cash at the end of the year, you would start the new year with $1,000 cash. Since the income statement is only for one year, you will start with zero in those accounts on January 1. For instance, let's say you paid $12,000 in rent last year. You will not have any rent on this year's income statement until you start paying rent this year.

Basis is the method used for the timing of such transactions and will affect when expenses will appear on your income statement. A *cash basis* is when transactions are only recorded when the cash is received or disbursed (spent). Individuals use this method, but it can also be used by some businesses. The other type of basis is called an *accrual basis*. The accrual basis records transactions when they are used, not when cash is received or disbursed. For example, a cash basis would record a 12-month subscription ($12,000) in the month it was paid, whereas an accrual basis would record one-twelfth of the total cost ($1,000) in each of the twelve months the subscription covers, even if it was all paid in one month.

#10 NET WORTH

DOWN:

1. Debt is listed as a _____ on a financial statement
3. When expenses are less than sales
4. A financial statement that shows assets, liabilities, and equity (also known as net worth) (2 words)
6. Money you owe

ACROSS:

2. Individuals use a _____ basis, which means income and expenses are recognized when money is received or paid
5. One way to increase your net worth is to buy assets that will _____
7. A financial statement that shows sales and expenses (2 words)
8. Something you own
9. Assets minus liabilities equals _____ (2 words)

24

Protecting What You Have

Insurance

You've probably heard many insurance jingles trying to convince you to buy their product, such as *"Like a good neighbor, (insurance) is there"* or *"Get (insurance) and avoid mayhem like me."*

So, what is insurance? Insurance is a way to protect what you own as well as plan for the future. Insurance companies sell policies (contracts) to their customers in return for premiums—the amount of money the customer pays for the policy. Insurance companies are permitted to invest money from the premiums. They may also sell shares of their company in the stock market to raise more money, or capital, for their business.

An insurance policy is designed to protect your assets by promising to pay you money to help you recover from a costly event such as a fire, theft, accident, illness, or death. When you purchase an insurance policy, you are transferring your risk of loss to the insurance company in exchange for the premium you pay. When you have an incident, such as a fire, you can file a claim telling the insurance company what happened and what you lost. When the insurance company pays your claim, as spelled out in the policy, they give you money to help you pay bills or replace belongings that were lost. One of the top five reasons for bankruptcy in the U.S. is medical bills. Although it is still possible, people with health insurance are less likely to go bankrupt for medical bills than people without health insurance.

In the section *Credit Scores*, I mentioned that people who have higher credit scores sometimes pay lower premiums than those who have lower credit scores. Credit scores are basically a risk rating. The lower your score, the higher the risk that you won't pay your bills, or at least, not pay them on time. Insurance companies may look at your credit score as a way of assessing how risky it is to write a policy for you. People who are careful with their money also tend to be careful in other areas. This is only one of the many factors insurance companies evaluate to determine their risk in issuing an insurance policy to someone. Age is another one. Young drivers have less experience than older drivers and tend to have more accidents, so they are more likely to cost the insurance company more money. Therefore, premiums are higher for young drivers. But when it comes to health insurance or life insurance, older people pay more because they are not usually as healthy as a young person and have shorter life expectancy, making them riskier to insure. The community where you live can also affect your premiums. If you live in a neighborhood with a higher crime rate, poor health, or somewhere more likely to flood, that will also drive premiums up because of the risk to the insurance company. Basically, the insurance company evaluates how risky it is to write an insurance policy for you, and that will determine whether they will write the policy and how much the premiums will cost.

Another consideration when setting the premiums on a policy is the deductible. The deductible is what you pay first before the insurance company must pay. For example, let's say you had a deductible of $500 on your renter's insurance policy. If the amount you lost due to a fire was $1,500, the insurance company would subtract your deductible from the total loss ($1,500-$500=$1,000) and pay you $1,000. Typically, if you set your deductible to a higher amount, the insurance company will charge less for your premiums. This is because the more you share in the cost of the loss, the less the insurance company will have to pay if you file a claim, which makes you less risky to insure. Most insurance companies also charge a reduced premium if you pay your full premium at one time, rather than at intervals throughout the year. This not only allows them to invest all your money in the beginning, but they also incur lower administrative costs involved in processing one payment instead of many.

Policies and premiums for all types of insurance can vary greatly from one company to another. Some insurance agencies sell policies for more than one company. The best place to start when searching for insurance is to ask people who are already insured if they have any recommendations. While it may be tempting to buy insurance online, that is usually not the best option. It is beneficial to work with an insurance agent you trust and choose an insurance company that has both financial strength and good consumer reviews.

DID YOU KNOW?

The premium or the price charged for an insurance policy should never be the only factor in choosing an insurance company. You want to make sure the insurance company you choose will be able to pay if you have a claim. Insurance companies are also rated. Companies like AM Best, Moody's, Standard & Poor, Fitch, and Kroll Bond Rating Agency (KBRA) analyze insurers' financial strength by giving them a Financial Strength Rating (FSR). Each company uses a different rating scale, but it is important when choosing an insurance company to pick one with a high FSR. This is an indication of the insurance company's ability to pay claims, especially if there is a widespread disaster like a flood, hurricane, or tornado.

Another way insurance companies get evaluated is through J.D. Powers and the National Association of Insurance Commissioners (NAIC). These companies look at customer service, customer satisfaction, reviews, and the number of complaints filed.

Let's look at some of the more common types of policies.

Auto insurance—Most states require people who own cars to carry auto insurance. An auto policy can have required coverage and optional coverage. Required coverage is liability insurance (insurance for any payments you would be responsible for if you had an accident) for bodily injury, liability insurance for property damage, and uninsured motorist coverage. There are normally other optional coverages you can add for an additional premium. An often overlooked aspect of insurance is the *duty to defend,* which states that the insurance company has a responsibility to represent you if you are sued after an accident.

Renter's insurance—States do not require renters to carry renter's insurance, but landlords often require renters to have a policy to rent. Renter's insurance protects you from loss of property in the event of fire or theft. Some renter's insurance will also cover loss of use if you have to temporarily find another place to live. It is important to note that the building owner's insurance only covers the structure and does not cover your belongings.

Homeowner's insurance—Homeowner's insurance is not required by any state or federal law. However, if you borrowed money to purchase your home, the lender will typically require it and that you name them as additional insured. This type of insurance includes *hazard insurance* (also known as dwelling coverage) and covers items like roof, walls, porch, and other structures (like a fence or shed), *personal property* for your belongings such as furniture, and electronics, *loss of use* (if you have to live somewhere else while your home is being repaired), and *personal liability* (if someone gets injured on your property or you damage their property) which includes medical payments to others. Homeowner's insurance usually comes with optional riders (additional insurance) for additional coverage. Note: it is important to insure your home for at least 80% of its replacement costs—

not its current value, but what it would cost to rebuild it. If you do not, you will be considered underinsured, and the insurance company may cover less than the full amount of your claim. A reputable insurance agent can help calculate the appropriate coverage for your home, as well as any additional coverages that might make sense for you to consider.

Private mortgage insurance (PMI)—This may be required if you borrow money for the purchase of your home and you pay less than 20% of the purchase price for your down payment. The premium for this insurance will be included in your mortgage payment, but it will not benefit you. This insurance protects the lender in case you default (don't pay) on your mortgage. Once you have 20% or more equity in your home—you owe the bank less than 80%—you can ask that the PMI be removed.

Umbrella insurance—This type of insurance is designed to prevent financial ruin if you are found liable for injury or damage to another person's person or property that is higher than the liability limits on your other policies. Umbrella policies are over all of your other policies (like an umbrella on a rainy day) and kick in when you have reached the coverage limits of your other policies.

Health insurance—Health insurance policies vary greatly. We covered health insurance a little bit in *Benefits*, because this is often offered by your employer as a benefit. If your employer offers health insurance, speak to human resources about what your policy covers. You can also get health insurance in what is referred to as the Health Insurance Marketplace at https://www.healthcare.gov if you are a U.S. citizen or national, or lawfully present non-citizen in the U.S. (see more information about eligibility on their website). If you are on medicare or are incarcerated, you are not eligible. There are also companies that will help you select an insurance policy from the marketplace. These policies vary in coverage and cost is based on your income.

Copay—This is a set dollar amount you pay for a particular type of service. If your copay is $35 for an office visit, then you will be charged $35 every time you visit your doctor. Often a copay for a specialist is more. Some policies require you to meet your deductible before you start paying co-pays. Other policies allow you to pay co-pays before you meet your deductible.

Deductible—This is the amount you will pay before your insurance starts to pay for things not covered by your copay. For example, if you go to your doctor for an office visit, and your copay is $35, you will only pay $35, and insurance will pay the rest. However, if you need an MRI, and your deductible is $2,000, you may have to pay $2,000 before your insurance pays any. Once you have met your deductible for the year, you will not have to pay for any services that would normally go toward your deductible.

Coinsurance—Most policies require you to meet your deductible before your coinsurance starts. This is the percentage of your medical bill that you pay, and your insurance company pays the rest. If you have 20% coinsurance and your bill is $100, you will pay $20.

Out of Pocket—Policies have an out-of-pocket maximum. This is the most you would pay in a worst-case scenario. You will continue to pay copays and coinsurance even after you reach your deductible until the total of your deductible, copays, and coinsurance reaches the out-of-pocket maximum. At that point, insurance will pay 100% until your costs reach your policy's maximum benefit limit, which can be annual, lifetime, or per type of coverage (such as prescription), renews, or changes in the next policy year.

In network—The copays and coinsurance apply to doctors in network, meaning the doctors who agree to accept your insurance plan. To be in network, they had to negotiate with your insurance company and agree to accept the rates the insurance company will pay for their services.

Out of network—There is usually an additional column on your plan summary that shows what percentage you will pay for out-of-network providers (this is sometimes 100%). These providers have not agreed to a negotiated rate with your insurance company.

No Surprises Act—This act was created to prevent charges from an out-of-network provider without your prior consent. Normally, you choose a provider in network, so your insurance will cover it. Here's an example of how this surprise could happen. You see your in-network doctor for an injury, and she sends you to get an x-ray—also in network. But the radiologist who reads the x-ray is out-of-network, so you get charged his full rate as an out-of-network provider. Out-of-network providers you did not choose are no longer permitted to charge you. For these types of out-of-network bills, payments now must be negotiated between the out-of-network provider and the insurance company. Emergency care is supposed to be treated as in-network. If you have any questions or disputes, you can visit https://www.cms.gov.

Life insurance—A life insurance policy is an agreement that when the insured dies, the insurance company will pay the face value of the policy to the named beneficiaries of the policy. This is intended to help pay funeral costs and unpaid bills and help provide support for the beneficiaries. The insured often chooses an amount of life insurance that is higher when the insured has a family they support. There are different insurance types even within the same broad category of life insurance. Be sure to do your homework or talk with an insurance agent to make sure you understand the pros and cons of each, as well as the impact on those you leave behind. Life insurance premiums also rise as you get older, so the longer you wait to purchase life insurance, the more costly it will be. Note if you have a life insurance policy that has cash value, pay particular attention to the terms of your contract. There are a number of factors that determine if the accumulated cash value will go to the beneficiaries or back to the insurance company upon the death of the insured.

> *Whole life*—This type of insurance is designed to last the insured's whole lifetime. It also has a savings component, known as cash value, which the policy owner can borrow from or withdraw. Withdrawals and outstanding loan balances reduce death benefits. This is sometimes used to help supplement retirement. Whole life has fixed premiums and death benefits.
>
> *Universal life*—This type of insurance is designed to last the insured's lifetime too and has a cash value component. Universal life has flexible premiums and a flexible death benefit.
>
> *Term life*—This type of insurance is designed for a specific time period. This type of policy has no cash value, so you cannot withdraw or borrow from this policy. Most people get this when they need some extra insurance for a shorter period, like when they have underaged children to support. This insurance terminates at the end of the period or if you stop paying the premiums.

Disability insurance— This is insurance to help with loss of income due to an illness, injury or medical condition that prevents you from being able to work.

> *Short-term disability*—This insurance is designed to help you pay your living expenses if you are temporarily unable to work due to illness, injury, a medical condition. The benefits are paid directly to you. Depending on your policy, you may be eligible for 40-70% of your normal pay before an accident or illness. There is usually a one or two-week waiting period before payments start, and disability coverage typically lasts until you can return to work—between thirteen and twenty-six weeks. Policies vary in cost, length of time, and the amount they pay.

Long-term disability—This insurance is like short-term disability insurance but doesn't start unless the accident or illness lasts beyond the short-term insurance period. It typically pays between 50-70% of what your normal pay was prior to the accident or illness. This is especially helpful to people raising a family. Policies vary in cost, length of time, and the amount they pay.

Long-term care insurance (LTC)—This type of insurance is designed to cover additional medical costs, in-home care, nursing home care, etc., and is typically purchased when a person is in their mid-fifties. An individual can purchase directly from an insurance provider that offers LTC, or it may be offered by an employer. To receive long-term care insurance, you must have physical or cognitive impairment, as defined in your policy. There is also a mandatory waiting period which is typically 90 days, although this varies among policies. Health insurance will not cover these costs, and this type of care can quickly deplete a retirement nest egg. The earlier a person purchases this policy, the less expensive it is. This type of policy often requires a health check to prove that the insured is currently in good health. A plan offered by the employer may have guaranteed issue, which means you would not have to be in good health to be covered. **Caution**: a long-term care policy purchased as a standalone *can be dropped by the insurance company* if it decides to no longer carry LTC. It happened to my parents, and the insurance company was not required to return the premiums they paid in, so they lost their money. I recommend anyone considering a long-term care policy consider an asset-based long-term care policy. This combines long-term care with a whole life policy, so an insurance company cannot drop the coverage. An asset-based, long-term care plan builds cash value over time, and the money can also be borrowed or withdrawn (rules vary among policies). The premiums for long-term care are expensive but can usually be deducted on tax returns.

Wills and Estates

Will—A will is a document that you use to say who you want to inherit your assets and act as a guardian for your children. A will is filed in probate court and is a public document. After death, a will always goes through probate court, and the court oversees any disputes. The will is carried out by the designated executor. There are many types, and wills should be discussed with an estate planning attorney to make sure it is done properly.

Trust—A trust also states your wishes in death, but a trust can be used during the life and after the death of the grantor or creator. Creating a trust is also more expensive than creating a will. The trustee is a fiduciary obligated to handle the trust assets by the terms of the trust document. Trusts are private and do not go through probate court. There are several types of trusts, and you should discuss with an estate planning attorney to make sure it is done properly.

BRAINSTORM:

What assets do I have protection for?

....

....

What are the deductibles on my policies?

....

....

Do I have protection against liability claims?

....

What could be the potential amount I may have to pay if someone sued me for a car accident or other liability?

....
....
....

What is not protected today?

....
....
....

What would be the cost if what is not protected now were destroyed or stolen?

....
....
....
....
....

If I have a car loan or lease, do I have GAP insurance in case of an accident?

....
....
....

I use or plan to use these insurance companies and they have this Financial Strength Rating (FSR).

....

....

....

Do I have a will or trust?

....

....

....

Do I have an estate planning attorney who can help me get a will or trust? If so, who?

....

....

....

Who are my beneficiaries?

....

....

....

#11 PROTECT WHAT YOU HAVE

ACROSS:

3. Life insurance designated for a specific period of time and has no cash value
4. The amount of money you pay for an insurance policy
7. Insurance companies are rated on this, which is an indication of their ability to pay claims (2 words)
9. Insurance will pay 100% after your deductible, co-pays, and coinsurance reach this limit (3 words)
11. Insurance designed to help you pay for your living expenses if you are unable to work due to illness, injury, or a medical condition
12. Medical providers are considered this if they have negotiated an agreed upon rate with the insurance company (2 words)

DOWN:

1. The amount of money you pay before the insurance company must pay
2. A contract designed to protect what you own
4. Unlike a will, a trust does not go through this type of court
5. A set amount you pay for a particular type of service, such as an office visit to your doctor
6. The percentage of your medical bill that you pay, usually after your deductible has been met
8. A person or organization that acts on behalf of another and is legally obligated to act in that person's best interest
10. You may be required to pay this type of insurance, which protects the lender (not you) if you put less than 20% down when you buy a house
13. A document that states who should inherit your assets and be a guardian for your children when you die

MAKE IT HAPPEN

25

Roadmap to Success

The secret of getting ahead is getting started. The secret of getting started is breaking down your complex overwhelming tasks into small manageable tasks and starting on the first one.

—MARK TWAIN, American humorist, novelist, and travel writer

So far, we have talked about earning, saving, and spending money. Now let's talk about what you want and how to make it happen. When we plan a vacation, we decide where we want to go and how we are going to get there. Then we tackle the small tasks like packing, booking lodging, and making travel arrangements before we start our journey. If we don't take care of the details, we won't have everything we need for our trip. It's the same in life; if we want to succeed, we must pay attention to the small tasks because each one takes us one step closer to where we want to be.

Skipping the small things is why so many people fail at accomplishing their goals. When people start with a big goal, achieving it can be overwhelming, which can sometimes lead to people giving up. Think about New Year's resolutions. Many people make them with good intentions, but according to a study at Baylor College of Medicine, 88% of those who make resolutions fail to continue with their goals after two weeks. Those of you who work out in a gym know how crowded it is the first couple of weeks in January.

It goes back to normal as people drop their resolve to work out. Their plans were just too big and overwhelming, and they failed.

When I first learned how to snow ski, I would stand at the top of the hill, look all the way down to the bottom, and feel overwhelmed (okay, maybe even freaked out). When I started down the slope, thinking about how far I could fall—I mean *ski*—I always fell. A friend told me to look only a few feet in front of me instead of all the way down the steep slope. *Hey, I could do that!* I could ski a few feet, and then a few feet more, and eventually I was able to make it all the way to the end of the slope. My big goal was to ski down the slope without falling. The key to my success was taking the slope a few feet at a time. I won't say I never fell again because I did, but I knew I could do it, and with some practice, I became better and gained confidence. When I stopped worrying about falling, I didn't fall as often. Each fall gave me feedback on what not to do as I learned how to get better. Life is like that. We can have big dreams, but we need to break them down into smaller steps to succeed. And we need to realize we will sometimes fall, that's how we learn and get better.

> *Life is not about how many times you fall down.*
> *It's about how many times you get back up.*
> —JAIME ESCALANTE, an American high school teacher

Dr. Gail Matthews, a professor of psychology at the Dominican University of California, conducted a study on which actions help us achieve our goals. The study participants decided what goals they wanted to achieve and were put into groups. The group with the lowest success rate of 42% did not write down their objectives. The group with the highest success rate of 76% not only wrote down their targets, but included action steps they would take. Also, they had an accountability partner—someone who would support and encourage them—with whom they shared a weekly progress report.

While there is scientific evidence that written goals are more likely to be achieved, these objectives should be clearly defined and intentional. Earlier, I shared that one of my workshop participants realized if her family gave up pizza night every other week, she could save about $50 per month. Let's look at how that might look stated as a written goal. A vague statement like "I want to save $50 per month" is not as effective as "I intend to save $50 per month by giving up pizza night every other week." Now she has stated her *intention*—not just wishful thinking—along with how she plans to accomplish her goal. And if she adds a reason why achieving this is important, she's more likely to stick with it. The objective is now, "I intend to save $50 per month by giving up pizza night every other week so I can save money and put my family in a better financial position." To help her identify even more with this goal and to remind her why she needs to accomplish it, she can create a vision board, adding pictures of what it will look like for her family when they are better off financially. Hanging this on the wall or posting it on Pinterest will remind her to keep working towards the goal.

To change our behaviors, we need to identify with the person we want to become rather than the person we are today. When I went through a divorce and became an unemployed, single parent of three young children, I fell into the trap of allowing society to define me. Society's definition of a single mom, especially an unemployed one, is not great. I read the statistics; single moms are usually poor, working two to three jobs to make ends meet, and they often slip into poverty. I even believed this for a while. Eventually, I decided that this was not going to be my life. I defined who I wanted to be and how our family's life would look. I told myself every day I was a financially successful single mom who could not only provide for her children, but could also give them the same things kids in two parent families have. My kids weren't going to do without. I had a goal, I had a purpose, and I now had a new identity. Because I constantly reminded myself of this new definition, I grew into it. It sunk into my subconscious mind and became my reality.

Simply having a clearly defined purpose you identify with is not enough to achieve it; you must list the actions you will take to succeed. These tasks are smaller goals that lead to the eventual accomplishment of your main objective. These smaller steps need to become habits. We all have good and bad habits, and they are often linked together to create a routine. For example, my routine may be wake up, shower, dress, eat breakfast, brush teeth, drive to work, grab a cup of coffee, sit down at my desk, and check emails. I didn't need a checklist to remember what to do next. The completion of each small habit is a cue for the next one to begin. Habits become part of our subconscious, and we do them automatically without even thinking.

So, the next step is to make a list of all the routine behaviors you need to add, change, or stop to achieve your target. For a habit you want to stop, try to unlink it from your routine. You need to get rid of the cue or substitute a new habit for an old one. In the example of the woman who wanted to eliminate pizza twice a month, maybe the cue to order pizza was when she drove past the pizza place on the way home Friday. She could change her route to eliminate that cue. If you want to stop spending so much money, you could make buying things inconvenient by only shopping when you are in the store (i.e., no online shopping) and only using cash.

When starting something new, remember to begin small to avoid discouragement. Try to link a new habit to an existing routine. Decide what will cue your new task to begin. We often do things in anticipation of a reward, so think about what would make you want to repeat this task. Using the example of saving fifty dollars a month by giving up pizza night every other week, she may want to start small by giving up only one pizza night per month. Because the family is normally anticipating a tasty pizza on Fridays, she could reward the new, no-pizza Friday with a favorite dessert or snack and have family movie night instead. Having something fun to replace the pizza night along with putting $25 in her savings the next day could be an incentive to continue with this new habit. Once the family gets used to this change, she could replace another pizza night and get to her goal of saving $50 per month.

After you continually repeat the task, it will become a habit. Some say it takes about twenty-one repetitions for a task to become a habit. Neuroplasticity is the brain's ability to change and restructure itself to learn and adapt. That is why the more you practice something, the easier it gets. When we try something new, our brain begins to restructure, kind of like building a new highway. The process is slow at first because it is under construction; we must consciously think about the habit. But once the highway is completed, you can zip right along. The habit becomes subconscious, and you do it automatically without giving it much thought.

If your ultimate objective is huge—like my desire to provide for my kids—you will need to create many small goals. It took years for me to get where I wanted to be (and a number of failures and a lot of prayers). If your main objective can't be accomplished quickly, don't be discouraged. Measure your success by accomplishing smaller goals and look at how much better off you are day by day, this month compared to last month, and so forth. Looking at where you are compared to where you want to be on a big goal can be like my experience learning to ski—overwhelming and scary. And sometimes the road to success can feel like two steps forward and one step back. The key is to define those smaller goals and celebrate your progress. I found it helpful to keep a journal of my little wins. It was rewarding and encouraging to look back and see how far I had come. If you want to create better habits, I highly recommend reading *Atomic Habits* by James Clear and *The 7 Habits of Highly Effective People* by Steven R. Covey.

DID YOU KNOW?

According to *Medical News Today*, foods that can boost memory:

Nuts and seeds	Dark and leafy greens
Salmon	Lean red meats
Beans	Avocados
Blueberries	Tomatoes
Whole grains	Red cabbage
Brown Rice	Green tea
Red wine and grapes	Dark chocolate
Quinoa	

Activities that may help increase neuroplasticity and improve cognitive skills and abilities:

Regular exercise	Learning to juggle
Stress management	Practicing mindfulness and meditation
Nutritious diet (see above)	Learning to use non-dominant hand
Lifelong learning	Painting or drawing
Good quality sleep	Coding computers
Mental health care	Playing video games
Learning new language or musical instrument	Traveling extensively and recording experiences

BRAINSTORM:

What habits do I need to get rid of?

....
....
....
....
....

How can I either unlink them from a current routine or make them more difficult to do?

....
....
....
....
....

What new habits will help me achieve my goals?

....
....
....
....
....

Is there a current routine I can link them to or a bad habit I can replace? If so, how will I make this happen?

....

....

....

....

These are my big goals:

....

....

....

....

....

....

For each big goal, list the smaller tasks or habits that need to happen to accomplish the big goal.

....

....

....

....

....

....

26

You've Got This!

Some people want it to happen, some people wish it would happen, others make it happen.

—MICHAEL JORDAN, American businessman and former NBA player

We have discussed many topics in this book. As I said in the introduction, this is not a how-to-get-rich-quick book. This is also not a book that is meant to be read only once. Read it and re-read it. Highlight things you want to remember. Make notes in the margins. Earmark pages you want to read again. This book is intended not only to be a financial reference guide, but also a source of motivation and encouragement to keep trying and learning. The more you learn, the more you will realize there is always so much more to learn.

*I have not yet arrived until I get the notion,
my knowledge is but a drop, my ignorance an ocean.*
— AUTHOR UNKNOWN

Always remember you are worth it. You have value and deserve to have a happy, successful life. You create a good life by knowing who you are, what you stand for, and staying true to your values and principles. Success happens when you are confident and understand you have the power to choose how to respond to any situation to create a better outcome. You are the author of your own life story. Believe that good things will happen for you and be willing to work hard. And most of all, share what you have. Be generous, kind, and respectful to others. They matter and are deserving too. Develop relationships with people who truly care about and support you and do the same for them.

> *A generous person will prosper;*
> *whoever refreshes others will be refreshed.*
> —BIBLE (NIV) Proverbs 11:25

You will have some failures. Remember that life always gives you the test before the lesson. In every failure, look for a learning opportunity that will take you one step closer to success.

Don't wait for everything to be perfect before you start. Life will never be perfect, so get up now and make it happen today!

> *What lies behind us and what lies before us are tiny*
> *matters compared to what lies within us.*
> -Ralph Waldo Emerson

#12 MAKE IT HAPPEN

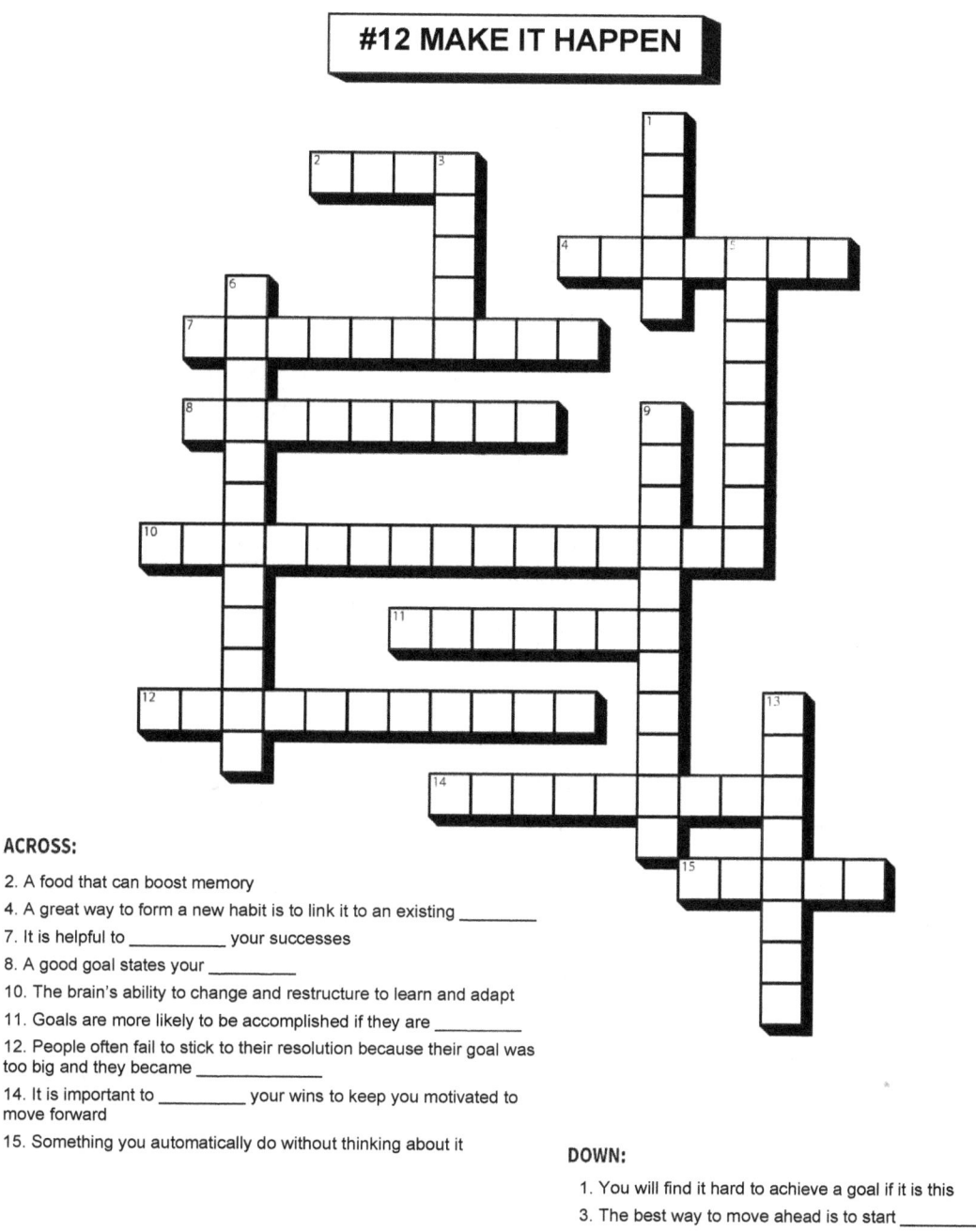

ACROSS:

2. A food that can boost memory
4. A great way to form a new habit is to link it to an existing _____
7. It is helpful to _____ your successes
8. A good goal states your _____
10. The brain's ability to change and restructure to learn and adapt
11. Goals are more likely to be accomplished if they are _____
12. People often fail to stick to their resolution because their goal was too big and they became _____
14. It is important to _____ your wins to keep you motivated to move forward
15. Something you automatically do without thinking about it

DOWN:

1. You will find it hard to achieve a goal if it is this
3. The best way to move ahead is to start _____
5. To change, we need to _____ with the person we want to become rather than the person we are today
6. An activity that can increase neuroplasticity (2 words)
9. This can be a helpful tool to remind you why you want to accomplish something (2 words)
13. Each failure gives us _____ on how to improve

NOTES

NOTES

NOTES

ACKNOWLEDGEMENTS

This book would not have been possible without the efforts of others to whom I owe a huge thanks! Thank you to my expert reviewers: *Lisa Block, CPFA®, CLTC®,* Partner, Regional Plan Services, Everhart Advisors, *Ron Cloyd,* Retired Senior Vice President, Huntington National Bank, *Mark Holsinger,* Chief Financial Officer, GLR, Inc., *Adam Horseman,* Client Relationship Leader, Montgomery Insurance & Investments, *Joan Mitchell,* Senior Vice President, Huntington National Bank, *Melinda Nigh,* Director of Human Resources, TCN Behavioral Health Services, and *Stu Schaffer,* Director of Finance, Benjamin Steel Company. I am grateful to you for fact-checking and suggesting additional content.

Thank you to my beta reviewers: *Wendall Bauman III, Alice Bourelle, Rachel Deitner, Lance Guisleman, Luke Guisleman, Melle Slager,* and *Debbie Simpson*. I really appreciate your input on how to make the book more appealing and relatable to teens and young adults. Your input on what sections were difficult to understand helped me know where to make things clearer.

A big thanks to Mary Vensel White of Type Eighteen Editing and Book Services for editing and coaching me through the publishing process. And last but not least, thanks to my daughter, Katie Baker of Greenwing Editing, who offered the inspiration for the book with her foster teen, encouraged me along the way, and provided editing and proofreading too.

PUZZLE ANSWERS

#1

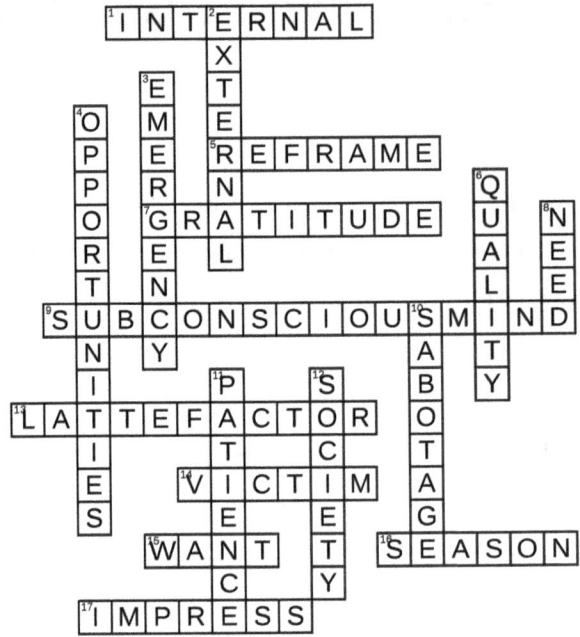

#2

#3

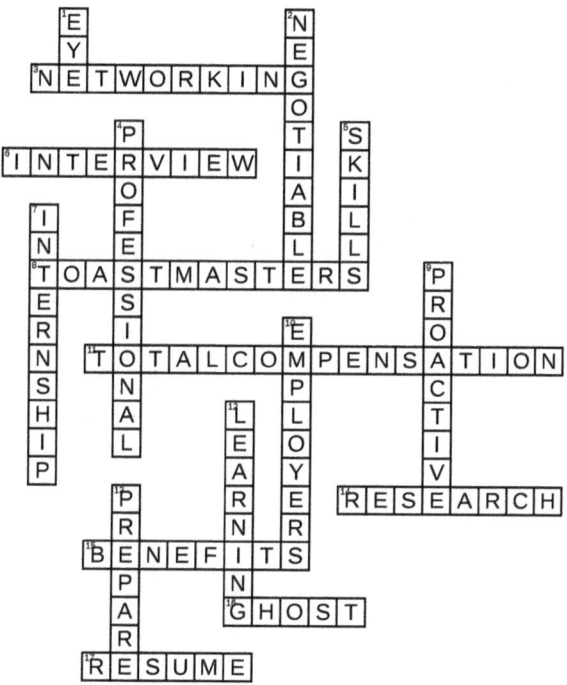

#4

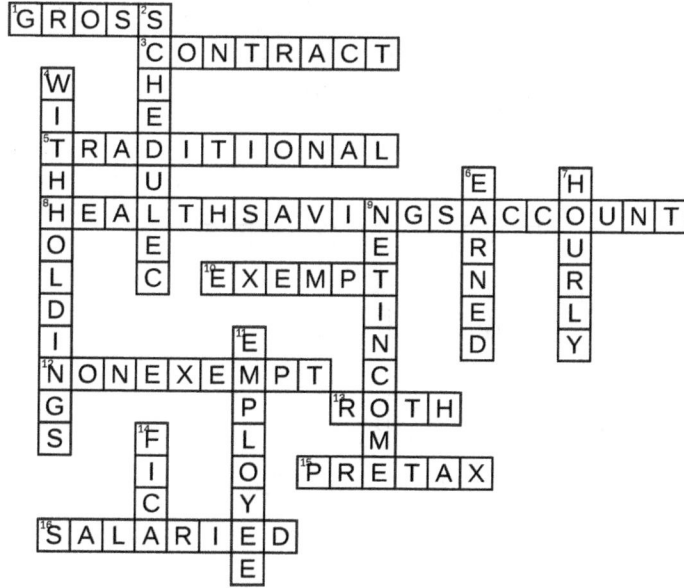

#5

#6

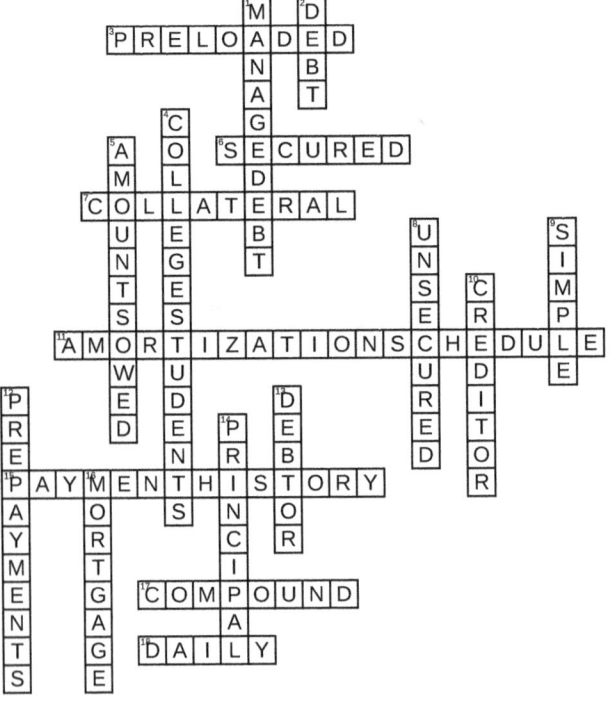

PUZZLE ANSWERS

#7

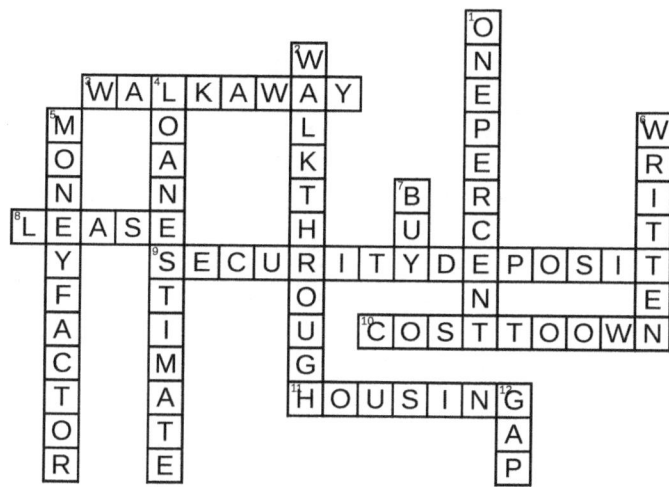

#8

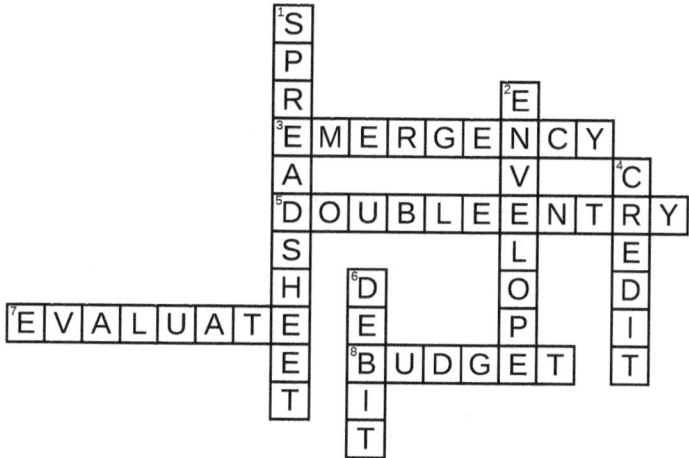

#9

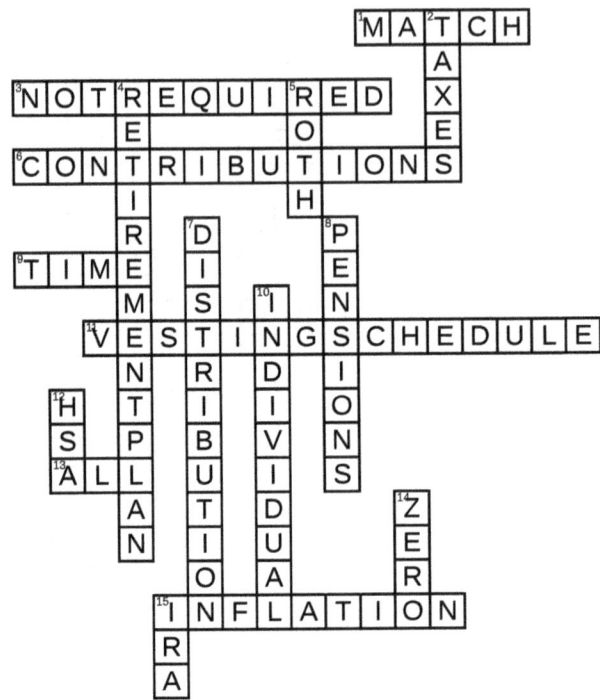

#10

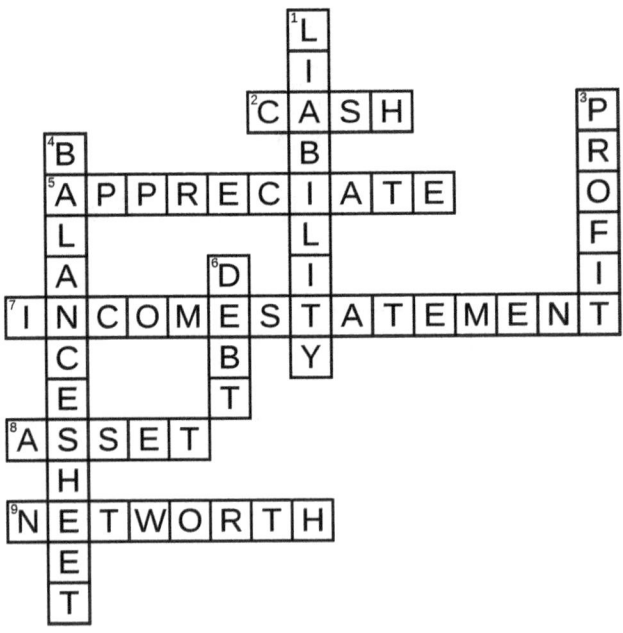

PUZZLE ANSWERS

#11

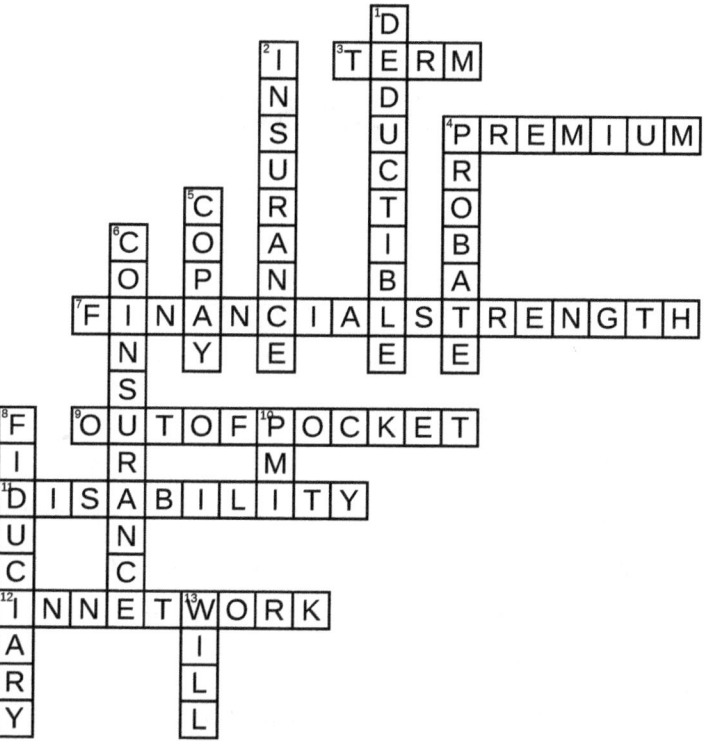

#12

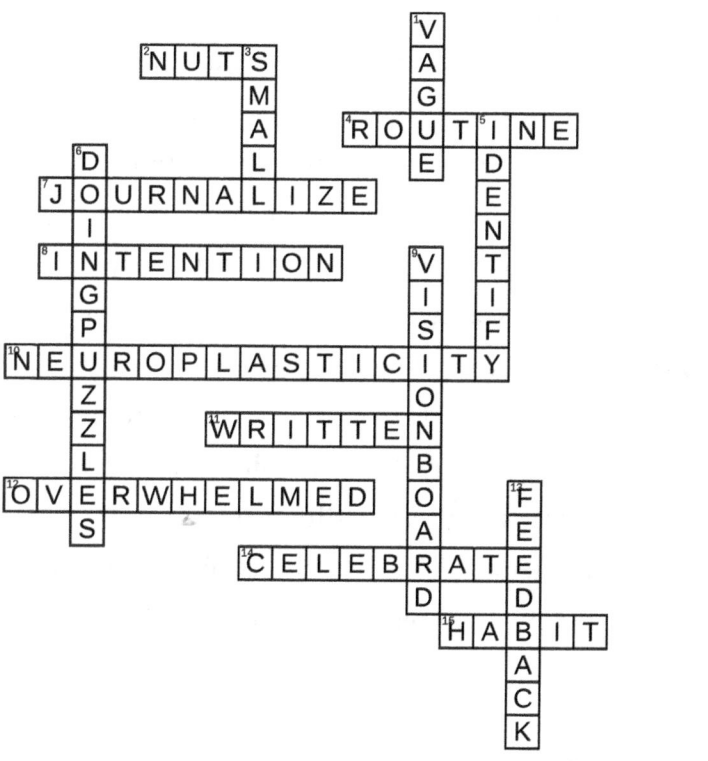

GLOSSARY

accrual basis: a method of accounting where income and expenses are recorded in the period in which they are earned or incurred regardless of when the money is received or paid.

accumulated depreciation: a way to account for the decrease in the value of an asset. It is listed on the Balance Sheet as a negative number. This is used for Fixed Assets that are expected to lose value as they age, such as a car.

amortization schedule: an accounting technique used to periodically lower the value of a loan or an intangible asset.

amortization calculator: used to calculate the monthly payment of a loan. It will also indicate how much of the payment will go to principal and how much will go to interest.

annual credit report: a report you can request from the credit bureaus to check for accuracy. The reports are free to request once per year guaranteed by federal law. Visit https://www.annualcreditreport.com.

asset: is something owned by a person or business, regarded as having value. Assets are listed on the balance sheet and have a debit balance.

associate's degree: is a two-year degree that you can obtain from a community college, junior college, online university, and some four-year institutions. An associate's degree of Arts (AA) and an associate's degree of science (AS) typically require 40-60 credit hours and is designed for people who are going to transfer their credits to a four-year college. An associate's degree of applied science (AAS) usually requires 60 to 100 credit hours and is designed for people who plan to go directly to a career.

Glossary

automated teller machine (ATM): machine where you can deposit or withdraw money using your debit card to access your bank account. Some charge fees and some do not.

auto insurance: an insurance policy to protect yourself and your car in case of an accident.

automatic payment: a scheduled payment that automatically comes out of your bank account to pay a bill or loan.

Automated Teller Machine (ATM): machine where you can deposit or withdraw money using your debit card to access your bank account. Some charge fees and some do not.

auto insurance: an insurance policy to protect yourself and your car in case of an accident.

automatic payment: a scheduled payment that automatically comes out of your bank account to pay a bill or loan.

bachelor's degree: an undergraduate degree awarded by colleges and universities after a student completes a course of study. A bachelor's degree of arts (BA) or bachelor's degree of science (BS) degree can be completed in 4-5 years and usually requires 120 college credits.

balance sheet: a financial statement that shows assets (what is owned), liabilities (what is owed), and equity (net worth).

beneficiary: a person or entity that receives money or other benefits from a person who dies.

benefit period: a period of time the benefit is in effect

benefits: a service (such as health insurance) or a right (such as vacation time) provided by an employer in addition to wages or salary.

bill pay: a service that allows users to pay bills online. It can be offered by banks, credit unions, and other companies.

bond: a debt security, like an IOU. Borrowers (like corporations or governments) issue bonds to raise money from investors.

budget: a spending plan based on income and expenses used to help businesses or individuals meet their financial goals.

C Corp: a for-profit business which has its own taxes separate from the owners.

calendar year: the accounting period January through December.

cap: capitalization or size of a company.

cash basis: transactions are only recorded when the cash is received or disbursed (paid). Individuals use this method, but it can also be used by some businesses.

cash projection: an estimate of cash that will come in and cash that will go out in the future.

certificate of deposit: a type of savings account that pays a fixed interest rate. Money must be kept in the account for the designated period, or you will lose interest.

Closing Disclosure and Loan Estimate (formerly called **Good Faith Estimate**)**:** a document that gives borrowers an overview of the estimated costs they will incur if they take out this loan.

Consolidated Omnibus Budget Reconciliation Act (COBRA): a benefit some companies are required to offer. This allows an employee who is no longer employed to be able to stay on their company's insurance plan for a period of time. Employees who were fired for cause are not eligible.

coinsurance: the percentage of your medical bill that you pay before your insurance company pays the rest. If you have a 20% coinsurance and your bill is $100, you will pay $20 and insurance will pay $80.

collateral: property the borrower gives as a pledge they will repay their loan. If the borrower does not repay the loan, the lender may take the property.

compound interest: interest paid on the interest already earned.

compounding frequency: how often interest is calculated.

condo fee: a monthly fee charged to cover maintenance and other expenses paid for by the condominium association.

contract labor: work based on a contract. A contract laborer is not an employee, but their income is considered earned income.

copay: a set dollar amount you pay for a particular type of medical service, such as an office visit.

cosign: someone who becomes legally obligated to repay a loan although the loan is made to another party. The cosigner can qualify for the loan and agrees in writing to pay off the loan if the primary borrower does not.

credit card: a card used to purchase items or services by borrowing money. The amount of the purchase will need to be paid to the credit card company. Purchases of this type are considered unsecured debt.

credit card statement: a listing of all charges and payments made on a credit card during the statement period and indicating the amount owed to the credit card company.

credit risk: the possibility that a borrower may not be able to prepay their loan.

credit score: a measure of one's ability to manage debt.

creditor: the lender of money.

current assets: assets that are valued at their actual value, like cash. They are called current because they can quickly and easily be sold for cash.

debit card: a card that is tied to your bank account. Purchases can be made as debit or credit, but the amount of the purchase will pull money out of your bank account.

debt: money borrowed that will need to be repaid.

debtor: the person or entity that borrows money.

deductible: the amount you have to pay before insurance will pay.

deflation: the general decrease in the costs of goods and services.

Department of Labor: a federal department that monitors the rules that govern labor in the United States.

disability insurance: insurance that helps if someone gets injured and can't work. This type of insurance can be either short-term or long-term.

distribution: money withdrawn from an account. Depending on the type of account there may be taxes and penalties.

dollar cost averaging (DCA): a phrase coined by Benjamin Graham which means if you are regularly investing, you will get a fair return on your money.

dividend reinvestment plan (DRIP): dividends received on investments that are used to purchase more shares of the investment.

earned income: money that your work for

education assistance: financial assistance for educational expenses, such as scholarships, grants, work studies, loans, or employer reimbursement programs.

EE: on withholdings represents what the employee is responsible for paying.

electronic funds transfer (EFT): money is paid or received electronically.

ER: on withholding represents what the employer is responsible for.

exchange traded fund (ETF): a group of stocks or bonds purchased for investors. These funds trade like stocks.

expenditures: payments of any type. These payments could be to buy assets, make loan payments, give refunds to customers, or to purchase goods or services, such as rent and utilities.

expenses: goods or services that are expected to be used or expire within a year's time, such as an oil change or utilities.

Free Application for Federal Student Aid (FAFSA): an application for students to apply for assistance with education expenses. Assistance may be in the form of scholarships, grants, work studies, or loans.

Federal Deposit Insurance Corporation (FDIC): an independent U.S., government agency that insures a financial institution's depositors' money up to $250,000 in the case of a bank failure. This insurance does not cover stocks, bonds, and other securities, crypto assets, life insurance policies, safe deposit boxes, or non-deposit investment products.

Federal Insurance Contributions Act (FICA): federal taxes deducted through payroll taxes (also charged through self-employment tax for contract workers). These taxes cover social security tax and medicare taxes. Employers are also charged for these taxes.

FICA medicare: part of the FICA taxes paid by employers and workers. Medicare is 1.45% and goes toward the federal health insurance plan for those 65 years or older or others with disabilities.

GLOSSARY

FICA social security: part of FICA taxes paid by employers and workers. Social security is 6.2% and goes toward retirement for retirees and disabled workers.

FICO: originally Fair, Isaac, and Co.is an American analytics company that analyzes data from lenders to establish a credit score for borrowers.

fiscal year: the twelve month period that businesses and organizations use for their financial year. Some entities use 52 weeks for their fiscal year. Individuals use a calendar fiscal year, or January through December.

fixed assets: items that are expected to last more than a year and have a value (usually of $2,500 or more), such as a vehicle or machinery.

GI Bill: a benefit for veterans that can assist with education, low interest loans, and securing a job.

gross income: the amount of pay before any taxes or withholdings are taken out.

health insurance: insurance to help pay for medical services and sometimes prescriptions too.

health savings accounts (HSA): an account that an employee and employer can put funds into to save for medical expenses. Must be on a high deductible health care plan in order to make contributions. This type of account grows tax-free.

home owners' association (HOA) fee: a fee charged by a community organization designed to make and enforce rules for the homes within the community and maintain common areas.

homeowner's insurance: insurance for the owner of a home to cover loss of dwelling and possessions, provide liability coverage, and additional expenses.

hourly wage: the amount paid to an employee that is paid according to the time worked.

in network: medical providers who have agreed to rates negotiated with the insurance provider.

incentive: something that encourages or motivates someone to do something.

income: money received

income statement: financial statement showing income and expenses.

inflation: a general increase in prices for goods and services.

informal education: a way to learn without going to college, such as through volunteer work, on the job training, reading, internships, listening to podcasts, or watching videos.

insurance: is a contract where you pay premiums in exchange for protection for what you own as well as plan for the future.

interest: an amount charged for the use of money. Loans charge the borrower for the use of the money loaned (principal) and financial institutions pay depositors for the use of their money.

interest rate: the percentage used to calculate the amount of interest on the principal amount borrowed.

internship: short-term work experience. They can be paid or unpaid.

individual retirement account (IRA): a tax-advantaged retirement account designed to help individuals save for retirement. These accounts can be either traditional or Roth.

irs.gov: the website for the Internal Revenue Service. A good place to find forms or look for answers to tax questions.

ladder: a savings strategy to spread cash across multiple certificates of deposit to take advantage of higher rates.

latte factor®: a phrase coined by David Bach, which refers to giving up a frequent, small purchase (a want) and putting that money toward savings instead.

lease: a contract that outlines the agreement between a person or entity who pays to use the property (lessee) and the person or entity that owns the property (lessor).

liability: something owed.

limited liability company (LLC): a corporation which protects its owners' personal assets in the case that the business gets sued. It can elect to be a pass-through entity like the S Corp, or it may choose to be taxed like a C Corp.

liquidity risk: the possibility that an individual, business, or financial institution cannot liquidate (sell assets or get cash) to pay off short term debts.

long-term care insurance (LTC): a type of insurance designed to cover additional medical costs, in-home care, nursing home care, etc., and is typically purchased when a person is in their mid-fifties.

massive open online courses (MOOC): providers such as edX and Coursera offer college courses for free or a low fee.

mortgage: a loan for the purchase of real property secured by a lien on the property.

mutual funds: a group of stocks or bonds purchased for investors. These funds do not trade like stocks and you cannot trade them frequently.

Myers & Briggs: a personality test that helps people discover what careers would be a good fit for them.

National Association of Insurance Commissioners (NAIC): a non-profit organization that sets standards for the U. S. insurance industry.

net income: income minus expenses, or profit.

net worth: financial worth. Assets minus liabilities.

no surprises act: an act created to prevent charges from an out-of-network provider without your prior consent.

non-employee compensation: a contract laborer's earnings. These earnings are recorded on a 1099-NEC.

out of network: medical providers who do not have negotiated rates with the insurance company.

out of pocket: the highest amount an insured will pay for healthcare in one year. After the out-of-pocket maximum is reached, insurance will pay 100 percent.

overtime: when an hourly employee works more than forty hours in a week. The amount over forty is paid at time and a half.

partnership: a formal arrangement between two or more parties to manage and operate a business. It also describes how the profits will be shared. There are three main types of partnerships: general, limited, and limited liability.

passive income: money received on investments or property you own. This is money you do not work for.

pay stub: a summary of an employee's gross pay, withholdings, taxes, and net pay.

payroll taxes: federal, state, and local taxes based on earned income and withheld from an employee's pay.

pension: a fund an employer regularly contributes to for an employee's retirement. An employee can draw from this fund when they retire.

post-tax: benefit payments that do not reduce taxes.

prepayments: paying more than the regular loan payment to pay off the loan faster to save money. Not all loans permit this.

pre-tax: benefit payments that reduce taxes.

principal: the original amount or remaining amount of a loan.

private mortgage insurance (PM): If the downpayment on a mortgage is less than twenty percent down, the buyer needs to buy this insurance which protects the lender.

prospectus: printed statement that informs prospective buyers or investors of something like a stock or fund.

paid time off (PTO): a benefit where the employee gets paid for time off for vacation, sick, or other personal reasons. The employer sets how many hours are permitted.

renter's insurance: insurance that covers the cost of belongings in the event of something like fire or theft.

required minimum distributions (RMD): this is the amount of distributions a retiree must withdraw from their retirement account beginning at a certain age.

retirement account rollover – direct: the money moves directly from one retirement account to another without the owner of the account ever having possession of the money.

retirement account rollover – indirect: when the money is moved out of the old account and sent to the owner, who then deposits it into the new account.

retirement plan: a plan the employer creates for employees to save money for retirement. These plans can offer traditional and Roth. Examples include 401k, 403b, 457, Simple IRA, and SEP IRA.

Roth: a retirement plan where money is taxed when contributed but nothing is taxable when it is withdrawn as long as the account is at least five years old.

S Corp: an unincorporated business with the one owner. There is no legal separation between the company and the owner. This is the easiest to establish and is popular for small businesses, individual contractors, and consultants.

salary-exempt: a labor classification that means a salaried person who gets paid the same amount each pay period regardless of how many hours they worked. Pay is based on completing the work, not the number of hours.

salary-nonexempt: a labor classification that means a salaried person who gets paid overtime for time worked over forty hours.

savings: a type of account that pays interest

Schedule C: a tax form for filing self-employment income and expenses.

scholarships: a payment made to assist a student's education awarded on the basis of academic or other achievement.

Securities and Exchange Commission (SEC): an independent U.S. federal agency created after the stock market crash of 1929 to enforce laws against market manipulation.

Sec 125 plan: named for a section of the tax code, and also known as a cafeteria plan, is an employee benefit plan that allows employees to choose from a variety of pre-tax benefits, such as health insurance.

Secure 2.0 Act: a law aimed at enhancing retirement savings for Americans by introducing various changes to retirement plans, such as raising the age for required minimum distributions.

secured debt: a loan that is backed by collateral, such as a car or house.

simple interest: interest is only calculated on the principal and not on interest.

Securities Investor Protection Corporation (SIPC): a non-profit member funded entity that returns customers cash and assets in the event of the failure of the financial institution.

sole proprietor: an unincorporated business with one owner. There is no legal separation between the company and the owner. This is the easiest to establish and is popular for small businesses, individual contractors, and consultants.

statement of cash flows: a financial statement that shows where the cash came from and where it went during a certain period of time.

stocks: securities that represents a fraction of the ownership of the issuing corporation.

subsidized federal loans: education loans that do not charge interest until six months after graduation

term life insurance: insurance on a person's life that is for a fixed period of time and has no cash value.

Toastmasters International: a nonprofit educational organization that builds confidence and teaches public speaking skills through a worldwide network of clubs that meet online and in person.

total compensation package: the value of pay and benefits offered by an employer to a potential employee.

trading account: an investment account where individuals can buy and sell securities, cash, and other holdings.

traditional IRA: an individual retirement account where contributions are not taxed. All earnings and contributions will be taxed when withdrawn from the account. There may also be a penalty if withdrawn before age 59 ½.

trust: an arrangement that states how your estate will be handled after your death. Can also be used during the life of the grantor. These agreements do not go through probate court.

tuition reimbursement: a benefit offered by some employers to assist employees in paying for their education.

umbrella insurance: insurance designed to prevent financial ruin if you are found liable for injury or damage to another person's person or property that is higher than the liability limits on your other policies.

unemployment insurance: assistance for workers who have been laid off or terminated (due to no fault of their own), so they can get money to help them while they look for another job.

Employers pay state and federal unemployment taxes, which is used to pay laid off employees.

universal life insurance: a type of insurance designed to last the insured's lifetime and has a cash value component. Universal life has flexible premiums and a flexible death benefit.

unsecured debt: a loan not backed with collateral.

unsubsidized federal loans: loans that begin charging interest as soon as you borrow.

US Treasuries: government debt instruments. Purchase of US Treasuries are loans to the federal government that they pay back with interest.

vesting schedule: a prorated way for an employee to earn access to certain employer benefits, such as retirement plan match, stock options, or a pension.

whole life insurance: type of insurance designed to last the insured's whole lifetime. It also has a savings component, known as cash value, which the policy owner can borrow from or withdraw.

will: a document that you use to say who you want to inherit your assets and act as a guardian for your children. A will is filed in probate court and is a public document.

withholding: an amount deducted from an employee's pay for items such as their cost of their benefits, child support, or garnishment.

work study funds: a form of financial aid that can allow you to earn money to help pay for educational expenses and gain experience.

workers compensation: designed to protect workers in case they get injured on the job. This is a tax paid by the employer.

RECOMMENDED RESOURCES

Books

Atomic Habits: An Easy and Proven Way to Build Good Habits and Break Bad Ones by James Clear

Atlas of the Heart, Mapping Meaningful Connection and the Language of Human Experience by Brené Brown

Bible: offers timeless advice on how to handle money

Build the Life You Want, The Art of Getting Happier by Arthur C. Brooks and Oprah Winfrey

Cash Flow Quadrant, Rich Dad's Guide to Financial Freedom by Robert T. Kiyosaki with Sharon L. Lechter, CPA

Change Your Thinking Change Your Life: How to Unlock Your Full Potential for Success and Achievement by Brian Tracy

Everyday Greatness: Inspiration for a Meaningful Life by FranklinCovey Co. and The Reader's Digest Association

Excuses be Gone!: How to Change Lifelong, Self-Defeating Thinking Habits by Dr. Wayne Dyer

Feel the Fear and Do It Anyway by Susan Jeffers, PhD.

First Things First by Stephen R. Covey

Leading at a Higher Level by Ken Blanchard

Multiple Streams of Income by Robert G. Allen.

Multiple Streams of Internet Income by Robert G. Allen

Positive Words, Powerful Results: Simple Ways to Honor, Affirm, and Celebrate Life by Hal Urban

RECOMMENDED RESOURCES

Practical Intuition: How to Harness the Power of Your Instinct and Make it Work for You by Laura Day

Principle Centered Leadership by Stephen Covey

Professionalism From A-Z by Clancy Cross

Reading People: How to Understand People and Predict Their Behavior—Anytime, Anyplace by Jo-Ellan Dimitrius, Ph.D., and Mark Mazzarella

Rich Dad, Poor Dad: What the Rich Teach Their Kids About Money—That the Poor and Middle Class Do Not! by Robert T. Kiyosaki with Sharon L. Lechter, CPA.

Secrets of the Millionaire Mind by T. Harv Eker

Smart Women Finish Rich by David Bach

Stop Saying You're Fine: Discover a More Powerful You by Mel Robbins

Strengths Finder 2.0 by Tom Rath

Stumbling on Happiness by Daniel Gilbert

The 7 Habits of Highly Effective People by Stephen R. Covey

The 21 Irrefutable Laws of Leadership by John C. Maxwell

The Butterfly Effect, How Your Life Matters by Andy Andrews

The Latte Factor by David Bach

The Power of One More by Ed Mylet

The Success Principles by Jack Canfield

The Total Money Makeover: A Proven Plan for Financial Peace by Dave Ramsey III

The Total Money Makeover Workbook by Dave Ramsey III.

What is Success by Jack Canfield

Who Moved My Cheese: An Amazing Way to Deal with Change in Your Work and in Your Life by Spencer Johnson, M.D.

Winning People Over: 14 Days to Power and Confidence by Burton Kaplan

Podcasts

Dare to Lead Podcast with Berne Brown
Mindset Mentor Podcast with Rob Dial
Simon Sinek—A Bit of Optimism
The Daily Motivation—Self Improvement with Lewis Howes
The Jack Canfield Podcast— Maximizing Your Potential
The School of Greatness with Lewis Howes
The Quote of the Day Show with Sean Croxton
The Tony Robbins Podcast

Websites

Jack Canfield: www.jackcanfield.com
Lewis Howes: www.lewishowes.com
Dave Ramsey: www.ramseysolutions.com

www.ingramcontent.com/pod-product-compliance
Lightning Source LLC
Chambersburg PA
CBHW080517030426
42337CB00023B/4554